Memoirs of an Anxious Teen
Freed from School Phobia

Memoirs of an Anxious Teen
Freed from School Phobia

Maëva Muratori

Original title: Mémoires d'une angoissée, guérie d'une phobie scolaire

Copyright © 2020, Maëva Muratori
All rights reserved, including partial or total reproduction, in all its forms.
www.phobiescolaire.fr

Edition: BoD - Book on Demand,
12/14 Rond Point des Champs-Élysées, 75008 Paris
Impression: BoD - Book on Demand, Norderstedt, Germany

© Cover: Coen Dalenoord. www.decreatiekamer.nl
© Photo: Brooke Cagle on unsplash.com

Scriptures marked ESV are taken from the THE HOLY BIBLE, ENGLISH STANDARD VERSION (ESV): Scriptures taken from THE HOLY BIBLE, ENGLISH STANDARD VERSION ®
Copyright© 2001 by Crossway, a publishing ministry of Good News Publishers. Used by permission.

ISBN: 978-2-9569337-3-1

Legal deposit: December 2020

Preface

While struggling with school phobia, I desperately looked for testimonies of people who had overcome it, but I never found anything that gave me hope. So I promised myself that if I overcame school phobia, I would write a book about it.

I want to thank:

Patricia, who translated the French version of this book into English.
Marcia and Jessica, who did an amazing job editing the book.
Coen who made the cover of the French, Dutch and English book.
And all those who encouraged me to share my story.

1
Birth of a Phobia.

October, 2009.

Monday morning, the first year of high school. For a month now, I have been getting up to go to class. Today is an ordinary day; however, something inside of me has changed. It feels like I am carrying a weight. A knot has settled inside my stomach and it makes me want to vomit. I can't eat anything and though I don't feel physically weak, I feel internally weak. I don't know why, but today seems impossible for me to face. I don't have the strength to attend high school this morning and pretend that I am ok. My mother reassures me that the feelings I am experiencing will eventually pass, but I wished that it would pass faster; much faster than that.

The plan this morning is for my mother to drive me to my school first, and then my brother to his. When we arrive in front of the high school, I feel stuck and unable to get out of the car. My throat begins to tighten and I feel like throwing up. When my mother notices that I am not feeling well, she drives my brother, Théo, to his school first so that I can have time to calm down. If only that would have helped...

Twenty minutes later, my mother and I are back in front of my high school and I still want to throw up. I have to gather all of my strength to get out of the car. I walk to a bench in front of the school entrance and sit down, but when I look at the school doors, it makes me even more nauseous.

Suddenly, I see a girl from my class who is, like me, late. I hurry to catch up to her and we enter the school building together. As we start to climb the stairs, she makes a joke about our English teacher, who will surely be annoyed with us for being late, but I can't even laugh because the closer I get to the classroom, the more I want to throw up. On the verge of fainting, I stop halfway up the staircase and tell her not to wait for me. I run down the stairs, heading in the opposite direction with only one thought in my mind: save myself. Run away! And the further away I get, the less I feel like throwing up. As I quickly flee out of the high school, it's like my life is at stake. I don't understand what is happening to me. Completely hopeless, I call my mother, crying. I am angry at her for making me come to school even though I knew something was wrong with me from the very moment I woke up this morning. My heart beats so fast, and my brain and stomach are turned upside down. It's like there is a little beast inside of me, pulling me back and keeping me from living a normal day.

I talk to my mother on the phone, and although she is not happy about me missing school, she asks me to go to my grandmother's house, which is only a five-minute walk from the school. My grandmother welcomes me with open arms and tells me, with her Italian accent, that it is good that I came to see her.

"When I was your age," she tells me warmly, "I also had days where things were not going good and that's okay. Sometimes the body says to stop because it just needs to rest."

Finally, someone who seems to understand me. I feel good in her house - it's a safe place. The TV is playing

Italian shows in the background and I already feel better. My desire to vomit has disappeared.

I spend that morning at my grandmother's house, and in the afternoon, I go back to school feeling a little apprehensive. As I walk through the main doors, I am afraid of feeling sick again, but to my relief, I feel ok. I go to my class, and everything seems normal again.

*

Thursday morning. It's back. I thought it was gone, but the little beast is back. My stomach feels tight, and I feel like I am going to throw up. The feeling is so strong that I rush to the bathroom, thinking that I am going to vomit, but because I didn't eat anything for breakfast, I don't have anything to throw up. As I sit in front of the toilet, I wait and stare into the toilet bowl. Today, just like on Monday, I don't feel strong enough to face the day. I have to take the bus to school, go to class, eat in the cafeteria, and come home by bus. These things seem beyond my strength. My first class today is gym class and I wonder how I am going to get there. As I sit on the floor by the toilet, I think to myself that I might feel better if I could just throw up.

Suddenly, my mother knocks on the bathroom door and asks if something is wrong. But I don't even know what to say to her. Annoyed, she tells me to hurry, as it is almost time to leave. Surprisingly, the thought of staying locked in the bathroom until it is too late to go to school comforts me. I force myself to get out of the bathroom and sit on the living room couch. I start to try to decipher what I'm feeling, but I don't understand.

"What is it, Maëva?" my mother asks.

"I don't feel good. I feel the same as I did on Monday."

"It's nothing, it'll pass," she reassures me.

"No, it's not nothing, Mom. I feel strange," I explain.
"Look, if you're sick, let's go to the doctor."
"No, I'm not sick. Actually, I don't know."
"Are you going to class today or not?" she asks me.
"No, not today. I don't feel like I can."

As soon as I know that I am not going to class for the day, the feeling of needing to throw up disappears, and I feel better instantly.

The next morning, I wake up with the same desire to throw up and the same uneasy feeling, reproducing the same scenario as the day before. This time, my mother, who doesn't know what to do, takes me to the doctor. On the way there I remain silent and, without knowing why, I feel strangely relieved that I am escaping a day of school. I have never had any problems at school and I have no logical reason to not want to be there…

As I sit in the waiting room, I am both nervous and impatient. Many thoughts race through my head. I think that my doctor might give me a few days off from school. I must be just tired; perhaps I've been overwhelmed with all of the changes from starting high school.

The doctor leads us into her office and asks us why we are there. She hasn't seen us in a while, which is generally a good sign. My mother explains the situation, and then the interrogation begins.

My doctor asks me, "Are you getting bullied in high school? Did someone ask you for money? Did someone hurt you? Are you being forced to do things you don't want to do? Are you sure no one's bullying you? Have you had sexual intercourse recently? Morning nausea for young girls is often a sign of pregnancy."

"No, none of that," I reply.

"You don't look so good," she continues, "You've looked much better before. Look, I'm going to give you a few days off, okay?"

I watch her write my medical note, sign it, and look up to observe me for a while. Turning toward my mother, she says to her, "Make sure she doesn't get school phobia because that would be a whole other problem."

*

My mind begins to race. How do you *'Watch out for a school phobia?'* Does someone struggling with school phobia have an alarm going off in their head saying, "BEWARE OF SCHOOL PHOBIA! BEWARE OF SCHOOL PHOBIA!"

How can someone avoid this? Is there a manual on how to avoid it and prevent it from settling in and chewing on one's stomach? Is there a way to stop it from taking control of one's brain and thoughts? These are all questions I will ask myself later.

In this moment, the only thing I can think about is the 15 days of rest the doctor has just given me. During these days, I will not have to fight with my parents or the little beast. Although I want to go to class and continue to have a normal life, I just can't do it anymore. Ever since the little beast entered me on Monday morning, it has started to take control of my life.

Just as the little beast attacked my high school life, it also attacked me at dance class, making me feel the same horrible things. As I attend what will be my last dance class, I sit in the corner of the class and watch the other girls dance. I am too ashamed and embarrassed to explain what is wrong to my dance teacher, so I lie and tell her that I feel sick. I don't want anyone to look at me. I just want to disappear into the walls and be forgotten.

During the fifteen days off of school, the feeling of the little beast burrowing into my stomach doesn't stop. The feeling never goes away – even while I do simple things, like go to the hairdresser. The little beast even holds me hostage at home. It is always lurking around, only manifesting itself when I go out in public. I don't want any of this. I don't want to stay at home and not attend school, but I just can't do it anymore. In my brief moments of clarity, I find my situation completely ridiculous and I tell myself that I will go back to school the next day. But in those moments of clarity, the little beast always wakes up and tells me that, from now on, it is the one who will make the decisions.

2

The Little Beast Settles In…

As my fifteen days of rest come to an end, the uneasy feeling remains. I know that I need to ignore what I am feeling, and tell the little beast to be quiet and to leave me alone so that I can go back to school.

I know that I can take the bus home *from* school, but I don't feel able to take it from home *to* school. So, when the day comes, my mother drives me to school. During the car ride, I anxiously squirm in my seat and my stomach aches terribly. The closer we get to the school, the more I feel like the little beast is waking up. My mother parks the car in the parking lot. The car is facing the school stairs, which are already filled with high school students whom we can hear from inside our car. She wishes me a good day and watches me, expecting me to get out of the car. But I remain stuck with my hand on the door handle.

"Are you going?" she asks me, nicely.

I feel the little beast gaining ground. It feels like it is crushing my stomach, moving up into my chest, choking me, and taking over my brain. Suddenly, I feel disconnected from myself, as if I no longer have control over my own body. Everything in me is controlled by fear and I feel totally insecure.

"I can't, Mom," I reply.

I feel like I am losing touch with reality. I don't feel like I can get out of the car, cross the courtyard full of people, and bear all of the people looking at me. It's beyond my strength.

"But why, Maëva?" she implores, "It's high school – you've always gone to school. I don't understand."

I can hear the helplessness in her voice and it worries me even more. I don't understand either.

The little beast takes this opportunity to infiltrate every corner of my body and I am drowning in the stream of thoughts that are buzzing around in my head. I feel like I am going crazy and that I am no longer me. I put my head between my hands and plug my ears so that I won't hear my mother anymore. What's happening inside of me is unbearable. Go away, you little beast! I want to scream and to tell it to disappear and to leave me alone. I want to escape school. I want to find a place where I can be left alone.

"So, what are we going to do, Maëva?" she presses, "Is it the same story as two weeks ago?"

Everything inside of me hurts. I want to disappear, disappear, disappear!

Breathlessly, I assert, "Take me to Grandma's."

"Taking you to Grandma's is not a solution!" my mother bursts. But she takes me anyway because she doesn't know what else to do.

Standing in front of my grandma's gate, the little beast quietly returns into its den. Feeling ashamed, I get out of the car and go to my grandma's front door. I feel so ashamed of my actions and embarrassed that I can't control this strange feeling. I want to escape the look of judgment from others, including my mother and my grandmother. I feel so ashamed.

Overwhelmed, my mother explains the situation to my grandmother, who listens calmly.

"Of course she can stay," my grandmother says gently.

"Her father will pick her up at noon," my mother says as she leaves to go to work.

Once I am inside her house, I calm down and forget about high school. As long as I am not confronted with school, the little beast stays quiet.

As expected, my father picks me up at noon. He doesn't understand my reaction either and is irritated. If I only knew what was going on, I could explain it to everyone! My Grandmother and Father speak in Calabrese so that I won't understand what they are saying. But I know that she is taking my side when my father ends the conversation with words I can understand, "No, she has to shape up – that's all."

We are completely silent on the drive home, which only makes me feel more uncomfortable. I hate myself for putting my parents through all of this. But little did I know, this is only the beginning of a long battle because the following days will be no different. Every morning is a continuous cycle – a cycle from hell. All I want is to go unnoticed, so I start dressing in ordinary clothes, tying my hair up, and no longer wearing any makeup. It doesn't make sense for me to wear makeup anymore since my tear-filled eyes would ruin it anyway. Yet, despite all of this, I have good intentions. Every day, I tell myself, *"Come on, tomorrow I am going."* But when the time comes, I have no strength to face it. I tell myself that I will go to school in the afternoon if I can't make it in the morning. But every time I try and go to school, I experience the same fight.

All day long, my mood changes abruptly, in a seemingly split second. To start, I am full of confidence, and I tell myself that I can do it and that I will do it. And then a second later, high school seems like an overwhelming obstacle. But nothing bad has ever happened to me at school to justify the way I am behaving. I am so terrified and I feel eaten away on the inside by the little beast who has proven to be stronger than me. I can't control it, I am a slave to it, and it takes control of my reasoning. One day, my mother tells me, "There are two of you, Maëva. There is a Maëva at home who is happy, and there is another Maëva who goes to school." This perfectly sums up my situation.

    I am not really aware of what is happening to me – I am kind of floating around, waiting for things to work themselves out and return to normal again. Every day is like a nightmare where I sink a little deeper into a black hole. My grandmother grows accustomed to me arriving at her house whenever I attempt to go to school. I often receive text messages from the class representative who asks me what is wrong and when I am coming back to school. *I DON'T KNOW!* My friends are also worried about me and I don't know what to tell them other than, "It's okay, don't worry… No, I am not coming this afternoon, but maybe tomorrow… No, don't wait for me." They are patient with me even though my answers are vague. Sometimes, I manage to go to class and try to make myself inconspicuous so that nobody will notice my presence. I just want to blend in. I want everyone to forget about me being there, and I don't want the teachers to question me because I don't want the other students to look at me. Other times, I only manage to spend the day in the library, desperately hoping that no one will find me.

*

    This morning, it is war again with my mother. She drives me to school because I can't get on the bus anymore. And today, like all other days, the little beast is choking me. Living a normal day seems beyond my strength. I am already running late for school because I have wasted so much time thinking, "*Will I get out of the car? No, I won't get out – Ok, I'll get out. No, I can't do it…*" My mother loses her patience when she realizes that it won't be possible for me to go to school today. She asks me to wait in the car. She says that she is tired of calling the school to report my absences and that she will go inside to report my absence this time. I feel the trap already.

"Mom, if you come back with someone to get me out of the car, I'm leaving."

I am terrified. My class is outside having gym class behind me right now. I feel like I would rather die than let anyone see me in this state. Minutes pass, and then, suddenly, I see my mother heading back with an education assistant. *Snap!* The trap is closing on me. My mother has told the education assistant that I am in the car and that I won't get out. This assistant has told my mother that she and I know each other well and that she can try to do something to help me. Filled with rage, I start to cry. I feel like everyone is against me. The education assistant tries to change my mind by telling me that I can stay with her and that together, we can eat some cake and talk. But I know that it is a trap. I know that I will be sent to class after I eat cake and talk with her. Then the little beast will become angry and it will hurt me. It will hurt me – not them. And they have no idea how mean the little beast can be.

I refuse everything they tell me without even listening to them. I don't want anything – no cake, no talking – nothing. She and my mom continue insisting for me to go with her, and I can feel the little beast, filled with impatience, growling and stomping around inside of me. I can't take it anymore. I get out of the car and start running toward my Grandma's house while my mother screams behind me, "MAËVA!"

I cross the pedestrian crossing without looking to the left or right. If a car ran me over, it would solve all of my problems. My mother drives up behind me and slows down to my speed. She is so angry, which only makes me feel even more oppressed. I want to disappear. I want a hatch to open up under my feet and swallow me up.

My mother demands, "Now that's enough, get in the car!"

I stop walking. I am not sure of myself or my actions anymore. Actually, I no longer know how I feel or what I should do. I am no more than a shell inhabited by a small beast. When my mother orders me to get in the car, my whole body hurts and I obey her without a word. I can't take it anymore. I want all of it to stop. As I sit in the passenger's seat, I don't know what she is yelling about because I am too focused on my suffering to notice her distress.

"You will explain the situation to Grandma! I'm late for work," she orders me as she drops me off.

Standing in front of my grandma's house, I think about what just happened. Now that I know that I am not going to school this morning, the little beast retreats into its den, gives me back my control and reasoning, and leaves me with a horrible feeling of shame. My grandmother greets me warmly and sits next to me on the couch.

"Maëva," she asks, "do you want us to pray to God and ask Him to help you to go back to school?"

Even though I may call myself a Christian and pray from time to time, God seems very, very far away. Especially right now. I accept her offer, but only to please her. I am so afraid to go back to class and face everyone staring at me. I just want to be left alone.

3
It Has Taken Over.

Today, we are celebrating my brother's birthday with my family. We have ordered our favorite apple and raspberry pies from the village pastry shop. These are the last beautiful days of October and we can still enjoy eating the pies outside on the terrace. I usually love birthdays with my family. It's always warm and it's also an opportunity to spend time with my cousins who are the same age as me. But this afternoon, I'm not feeling well. It is Sunday and tomorrow is Monday. Monday means class; class means high school; and high school means the little beast. I can't enjoy my Sunday or my family because that's all I can think about.

With a piece of pie in my hand, my cousin and I sit behind the house to eat and talk quietly, but I'm not hungry. My throat is tight and being surrounded by people oppresses me, even though it is only my family. I don't want to be asked what's wrong and why I don't go to school anymore because I don't know the answer either. My grandmother is here, too. I appreciate her discretion and the fact that she has never asked me these kinds of questions.

While thinking I'm safe from interrogation, my cousin starts questioning me.

"Are things not going well at school?" she asks, suddenly.

Catching me off guard, I reply, "Is this a joke?"

"My mother told me to ask you. Your mother is worried. Did somebody hurt you, or were you asked for money?"

"No!" I insist, "Why is everyone so persistent about this? I just want to be left alone!"

"But it's bad, Maëva. Why don't you go?"

I can't explain the feeling that I am experiencing. It's like I'm a slave. All I know is that I have this unreasonable fear that has paralyzed me ever since the little beast came into my life on that Monday morning.

*

As strange as it may sound, it has almost become reassuring to feel the little beast right from the moment I wake up before school. It means that I will be too afraid to face a day of school, and that my fear, by taking over my mind, will make me stay home.

This morning is no exception. After telling my mother that I don't feel like I can go, I am overwhelmed by terrible guilt but, at the same time, I am relieved to not have to fight with her or the little beast. I would like to go back to school, please my parents and stop worrying them, but I just can't.

After saying goodbye to my mother as she leaves for work, I grab my computer and start writing again. This is all I can think about anymore: writing, writing, writing, writing. Writing to forget, writing to escape this daily life, writing to calm down.

I have been writing a story about friends who lose contact and meet again a few years later, which strangely echoes my story. I began the story when I started to stay home from school, and at least while I write, the little beast leaves me alone. This is all I'm asking – that I'm left alone and not asked any questions that I don't know how to answer.

Suddenly, the phone rings. At the other end, I hear a voice I've heard before.

"Hello, Maëva, it's the high school nurse."

My blood falls to my feet and I feel sick. Just having the nurse on the phone connects me to high school and I can already feel the little beast waking up.

"It's been a while since you've been here. Maybe it's time to slowly come back," she says encouragingly, "What do you think? I suggest you come through the infirmary instead of the main entrance; it leads to the back of the courtyard. There's a little path on the right just before the parking lot where you can walk up to the top and I can come and open the gate for you. Okay?"

She waits for an answer.

What am I supposed to say? Should I tell her that it's fine with me? *But no, it's not fine at all! Why is everyone coming after me? Why don't they just leave me alone? I'm not asking anyone for anything, I just want to be left alone!*

"We'll meet this afternoon?" the nurse persists.

What, today?! I'm going to go to school today? The little beast is upset and gets louder and louder. I feel bad before getting there.

A weak, "Alright," comes out of my mouth without me knowing how.

"All right, then," the nurse confirms, "I'll see you later."

I'm still holding the phone up to my ear when the tone ending the communication resounds. I'd like to tell her that I've changed my mind and that I don't want to go anymore. I'm doing very well on my own, thank you! But it's too late, the appointment is made. The little beast is really not happy and has already started crushing my stomach. I just want to scream. I want to scream at the little beast, tell it to stop hurting me, and cry.

Upset, I call my mother at work. She seems rather calm and thinks it's a very good idea. I don't! Does anyone care about what I think? I think it's a very bad idea. I want to be left alone. I want to be left at home and not asked any more questions. That's the only way the little beast will leave me alone.

I'm counting the hours, minutes, and seconds before the fateful hour. At noon, I'm not hungry. The little beast is sitting on my stomach, ready to make me regurgitate anything I swallow. Until now, I had the situation under control, but today I have no choice and that's what terrifies me. The clock's hands are moving too fast and I want to rip them off.

As she picks me up to drive me to school, my mother asks if I packed my bag. My bag? What bag? The deal is to go to the infirmary, not to school! I already don't feel like I can walk through the school door. I grab my bag without knowing what's in it, and I don't care because I only take it to blend in.

In the car, I can feel that the little beast is awake and that it has gained strength during the last few weeks I have spent at home. It is everywhere all at once: in my stomach - twisting my guts; in my legs - taking away my strength; and in my brain - telling me that it will all go wrong and that I shouldn't go. The closer we get to school, the more ferocious it gets. By the time we get there, I can't take it anymore.

"Mom, I can't," I can barely speak out.

My mom parks behind the big building on the side of the infirmary and encourages me not to give up when I am so close to the goal. I'm going to die. My legs aren't responding and I feel like I'm going to faint. I stare at the little gate the nurse told me about on the phone. Through her office window, I can see her getting up to meet us. I don't feel like I am going to be able to get one foot out of the car. If I get out of the car and go through that gate, I won't be able to go back – I'll be trapped. My mother comes to open my door and takes my bag to encourage me to get out of the car. I can hardly force myself to get out, and the little beast is furious.

"Mom, I don't feel well. I feel like throwing up."

She doesn't listen to me.

"Mom, I'm really going to throw up," I insist as we walk forward.

Every step I take brings me closer to my prison and condemns me a little more. I just want to sit there on the pavement and let the ground open under me to swallow me up.

When the nurse opens the gate for us, I feel like a death row inmate. My mother has told me many times that I'm not going to prison, and that it's only high school, but I feel like going to prison would be less terrifying. I want to run away. I want to run very, very far away. But where would I go? Nothing will get me out of this dead-end.

I timidly respond to the nurse's greetings as she invites us to follow her. I want to go home. My mother gently pushes me forward with her and when I turn around, I can see the gate closing behind me. In the distance, I hear noise from inside the school windows and I am terrified that people I know will see me like this. I don't want to be here, I don't want anyone to help me. *I've changed my mind, and I feel fine! That's right, let me go home and we'll see about this tomorrow.*

The nurse leads us into the infirmary and I smell a mix of odors from a medical and dental office. She welcomes us into her office and tells me to sit down, but I want to get up and run away. But where would I go? When my mother thanks her, says goodbye to me and leaves, I start to panic. The little beast bites me and it hurts – it really hurts. I feel like I'm going to cry. I look for comfort from somewhere, but nothing here is familiar to me.

The school bell rings and the little beast rages inside of me.

It gets even more mean when the nurse asks me, "Are you going to class?"

I want to scream! Suddenly, my heart races as I desperately try to calm my breathing. I want to tell the little beast that it's really hurting me and that it should stop and let me breathe once in a while. I feel trapped and betrayed, as if the nurse was in cahoots with the little beast. I didn't come for this. I came here because she asked me to, but going to class wasn't part of the deal!

"Wh-what? No, I can't..."

To my relief, she doesn't force me to go. I stay in her office all afternoon. We talk a little, but I still can't answer, 'Why can't you go to class anymore?'

I see a few people come into the infirmary. They don't understand why they are told that they can come in when I'm already sitting in the infirmary office. I feel uncomfortable and out of place. But what worries me the most is how I'm going to manage walking through the school to get to the bus. I think of shortcuts in my head, possibilities to escape being seen by others, and especially ways to avoid anyone I know. I'm afraid of the famous question that I don't know how to answer. But the answer is simple: *I'm afraid of school.* And that's the answer I'm ashamed of and that I can't tell people because being afraid of school at 15 doesn't make sense to anyone.

The moment that I've been dreading from the very beginning starts when I hear the school bell ring. I take my bag and say goodbye to the nurse who has been patient with me. In the school courtyard, I feel like I'm about to enter a lion's cage, ready to be eaten. This would be a legitimate feeling if I had been assaulted or harassed, but I hadn't experienced any of that. I take a deep breath when I feel the little beast. The entire time I'm in school, it twists my intestines with its hairy paws and it only leaves me alone when I get home. It's not happy now, but I don't care because I know that once I get out of here, it'll go back into its lair.

Everyone is already in the lobby by the time I walk into the school. I lower my head, and without looking up, run down the stairs as fast as I can, knowing that my ordeal is almost over. The little beast is already starting to let go of me once I reach the parking lot. I stand far away from everyone while I wait for my bus, desperately hoping that no one I know will see me. If only I could camouflage myself to blend in with the scenery. I wait until everyone has gotten onto the bus and when they are all settled in, I get on without even bothering to look for a place. I just sit in the first free seat, making myself very small and completely turning my face toward the window so that the next students who come on won't see me. When the bus starts, I'm exhausted. I feel like I have been running a marathon since the beginning of the afternoon, which has only now ended. This is the first and last time I will do this. The nurse set up another appointment with me tomorrow, but I won't come back. There's no way I'm going through a day like this again. Satisfied with this conclusion, the little beast enters its den and lets me forget about its existence, leaving me alone with questions. Why, why, why?

*

I now fear the night because of the little beast that has taken over my life. I hate being alone in my bed, in the dark, confronted with that mean little beast that terrorizes me about tomorrow. Filled with fear, I cry into my pillow, but my crying wakes everyone up. My brother sighs in his bed and my father has lost his patience. He comes down the hall and opens my door wide.

"Now you stop!" my father demands, "Mom and I are working tomorrow, and your brother is getting up to go to middle school. You're not alone in this house!"

He heads back to bed, slamming my bedroom door and leaving me alone in the dark with the little beast. I'm like a little girl who's afraid of the monsters under her bed, except I'm not a little girl anymore and the monster is inside of me.

The problem is that I think too much. My mother often tells me that I have a little bike in my head that pedals all of the time and that I should stop it. I imagine everything, even the unimaginable, and that's what stops me from living life.

I'm afraid of being afraid. I'm afraid that I will be afraid for the rest of my life. The everyday little things like taking the bus or going to an appointment have become difficult. I see my day as a number of obstacles to overcome. It's a constant battle of fighting against the little beast inside of me and it's tiring. It gnaws at me all of the time and it hurts me so much that there are times when I think that dying would be better than going through this. I don't have any suicidal thoughts, but it's so unbearable that sometimes I just don't feel strong enough to face it. It exhausts me and drains me of all my strength. I'm tired. It's not a physical fatigue, but a mental fatigue. I'm tired of living. I am in constant confrontation with the little beast that has settled inside of me and it does not want to leave. I feel vulnerable and terribly lonely. No one can understand what is happening to me, not my extended family, not my parents, not my brother. Not even me.

*

The days go by and they all look alike. My high school life is like a prison sentence. I went back to school the next day because, according to my mother, now that I had set foot in high school again, giving up was not an option.

This is how I have ended up in the school infirmary over the last few days. It has become a habit. At 8:15 a.m., we park at the back of the school and wait for the nurse to come and open the gate for us. Every time, I beg my mother to take me home, but she won't give up. At night, I tell myself that dying would be better than facing another day. The little beast, who has settled into my stomach, never lets go and devours all of my will. I don't even want to make an effort to get up anymore – it's too hard. But I am not given a choice. I would give anything to be left alone.

When the nurse arrives, my mother accompanies me inside the infirmary and then goes to work, and I find myself alone with the nurse and the torturous little beast inside of me. At noon, since I am unable to enter the cafeteria, one of my parents brings me home to eat and my mother takes me back to school in the afternoon. It's a routine but not a peaceful one. Every morning and every afternoon is a nightmare that starts again – a nightmare that I have to face twice a day. But it's the only solution we've found so far.

For the first few days, I stay in the infirmary. Even when the nurse has to leave, I sit alone in the little room where I am sure no one will find me. Sometimes students come into the infirmary with a fake headache hoping to skip class. When they ask what's wrong with me, I want to say that school makes me sick. But instead, I invent a stomach ache or mumble something incomprehensible so that they will leave me alone. The less people talk to me, the better I feel. I feel like I'm being held accountable to give them an answer to the question, when I can't even answer it myself.

This continued for a while, but eventually, I knew things had to change. Before I can tackle the problem of going to class, I have to get used to being on the school campus surrounded by other students. I can walk through the building to the bus parking lot because I know that I'm going home. But going to the center of the high school and staying there is another obstacle. To start, the nurse and I go to the common area, but avoid going during the busy hours. I'm more than afraid of running into my friends, who don't understand what's happening to me, or other acquaintances who might ask me *THE* question.

When being inside of the high school is no longer much of a problem, we try going to class. But the result is discouraging. I am paralyzed at the thought of being in my classroom. I haven't been there in such a long time and I know that I will be asked questions, *THE* question, the one I fear so much. In a class of thirty students, no one usually pays attention to this kind of thing, but over the months, we get to know each other, and we know who is there and who is not. And, for "Maëva", yes, the students are used to hearing she's absent.

I try my best to go to class, but the little beast protests. The closer I get to the classroom, the more it takes control of my reasoning and usually I am forced to turn around because I can no longer think properly. Sometimes I manage to suppress the little beast enough to go to class, but it's always there, ready to pop up if I let my guard down a little too much. Going to school remains a big, unresolved problem and the nurse, who is so patient and kind, is starting to get worried.

"Maëva," she gently nudges, "you know that if you don't do something about this, you'll have to be hospitalized. Is that what you want?"

This stuns me. Hospitalized? When she says this, a picture of myself lying in a hospital bed, intubated and with an intravenous line in my arm pops in my head. Why would anyone want to hospitalize me? I'm not sick.

4
Help!

A child psychiatrist. Since something has to be done, this is the first thing we try. One evening, my mother sits on the edge of my bed and asks me what I think about a child psychiatrist and if I think it would help me. Not wanting to refuse what I am offered, I accept, but I feel awkward. *Only crazy people go to a shrink, right?* Recently, a friend told me, "When we see you, we don't think you're sick." I don't feel sick or crazy, rather just out of touch with people my age. I feel too mature with some things and not mature enough with others.

My first appointment happens to be on my mother's birthday. *Happy Birthday, Mom.* The whole family makes the trip: my parents and my brother, who has brought his game console to keep himself busy, are here with me while a stranger processes my case. I have no idea what to expect and the little bike in my head keeps pedaling. Do psychiatrists carefully observe our actions and gestures to know what we think?

The waiting room is a strange place with weird paintings, geography books, children's books, comic strips, and newspapers. When the psychiatrist comes out of his office to get me, I find him just as strange, wearing sandals with socks that go all the way up to his mid-calf. In the consultation room, the shelves are full of Lego boxes, toys, little trains, plastic dinosaurs, and dolls. The walls are covered with thick carpet and there are so many things in here to reduce the noise that I can't even hear myself dragging my feet on the carpet. I walk around a small table with paper and pencils and sit on the edge of the couch filled with stuffed animals. A child would certainly be happy in the middle of all this, but at 15, I've outgrown this. All this stuff around me doesn't amuse me at all and some of the stuffed animals look creepy. On one of the shelves, a clock has a different kind of bird on every hour and it makes a ticking sound. What have I gotten myself into?

The psychiatrist starts by asking me the usual questions: what is my name, what is going on with me... Then nothing happens. He occasionally asks me a question, but what we hear most during the forty-five minute appointment is the ticking of the clock and my stomach growling. The moments of silence are quite embarrassing, but maybe it is a technique used by mental health doctors to analyze their patients.

Up until the end of the school year, I am followed by this child psychiatrist, who tells me that my school phobia can leave as quickly as it came. "Sometimes all it takes is a little click," he explains. Besides, according to him, I'm better and almost cured. But if it was as simple as a little click, this little click would have happened by now, right? And I know I am anything but cured.

*

After many failed attempts to go back to school, we have an appointment with the school principal to discuss my case. With my parents, I climb the big staircase leading up to the main entrance, feeling like everyone is looking at me and that everyone *knows*. Jokingly, my mother asks me if I'm ashamed of my parents. No, I'm not ashamed of my parents. I'm ashamed of myself; of what's happening to me.

"I don't care," I mumbled, "I won't see these students again."

Today, I'm not afraid of other people staring at me because this is the last time they will see me. Sitting in the principal's office, he says exactly what we expected: I can no longer attend high school because my absences are too frequent; we'll have to find something else until I'm able to resume classes normally.

There. Are you proud of yourself, little beast? What am I going to do now?

My parents feel helpless and I am ashamed to feel relieved. The decided backup solution is the CNED, correspondence courses, which are free until the age of 15. But the CNED for a school-phobic is like painkillers for a cancer patient. It reduces the pain, but the problem is still there and it progresses and gains ground. Additionally, even though the psychiatrist has warned us that it may cause me to self-isolate, it's the only solution we have.

My father decides to confiscate my computer in the hopes that depriving me of it would make me go back to school. To deprive me of my computer is to deprive me of my virtual life and everything surrounding it.

Since the beginning of my high school years, I have been a fan of a music band, TH, and could spend hours watching their videos on the internet, reading their blogs, reading articles about them, and looking at their pictures. My bedroom walls are covered with pictures of them. I know all their songs and my life revolves around them. I eat TH, I sleep TH, I speak TH. I know my dad doesn't like this band. He doesn't like what they sing about and he really doesn't like that the name of the band was "Devilish" (Diabolic) before they changed it. But I don't care, I love them too much.

Being without a computer is not as difficult as I thought it would be, even if it was my only hobby. Writing, writing, writing, that's all I have left now.

5
A Breath of Fresh Air?

I am officially enrolled at the CNED. While I wait to receive my books by mail, I am pretty relaxed; I have my life at home, far away from high school. Since I no longer need to go to school, everything is fine; it's as if there has never been a problem. Already, my mother and I have set up a timetable where the different subjects are spread out over the year. It wasn't easy, but we did it. All I have to do now is stick to it and work: do my lessons, do my homework, and send it to the teachers to correct it.

In the beginning, it works pretty good. I'm serious, I focus on what I have to do, I learn my lessons, I do the exercises, and I send in my homework.

And then very quickly, I lose track.

As soon as I get stuck on an exercise and look up from my notebook, something steals my focus. My father has given me my computer back because I need it for my lessons, but I get easily distracted on the internet. Then there's my cell phone, the TV, my camera, the magazines lying around, my cat sleeping on my bed... He's got a good life. Sleeps all day, has no worries, happy with a bowl of cat food and some attention. I would like to be a cat to escape this life.

Every Tuesday afternoon, I meet my high school friends who have a free hour in their schedules. I think it is reassuring to my parents that my friends and I keep in touch because I don't see many people now that I'm doing correspondence courses. We sit on a bench and talk for an hour in front of the school without it being a problem for me.

As time goes by, I even manage to enter the school through the main doors. As long as I don't have to go to class, everything is fine.

*

Saturday afternoon, I wake up from my nap to find someone sitting on the edge of my bed. My head is still a little foggy and it takes me a while to realize that it's my aunt, Sandrine. I wonder what she's doing here.

"Maëva," she starts, "I have to tell you something."

I don't remember her ever speaking to me in such a serious tone. I tell her that she is scaring me. What? What's going on? Did something happen to my cousin? I am immediately overwhelmed by panic.

She tells me that she is taking antidepressants right now and that she suffered from one of the side effects last night. She describes how she threw up and had a cold feeling creep up into her arm, as if she was dying. But as soon as she clung onto her husband, who is a Christian, the cold feeling went away.

"I prayed all night to not have to take these antidepressants anymore, and, I don't know why, but I saw you. Maëva, you've got to pray and you're going to be alright. God told me that it's Jesus who will save you."

She starts crying and so do I. It's so strange that I don't even know if I'm still sleeping or if I'm awake. When she hugs me and says she loves me, it makes me cry even more.

*

I wasn't making any progress with the child psychiatrist, so my parents suggested that I should go see another one. Sitting in the waiting room of a new psychologist, under the leaves of a plastic plant, I'm not feeling very comfortable. I want to disappear. The little beast, not happy at all, gnaws at my insides and whispers to me that I should go home.

"Mom," I plead, "I don't feel well, I want to go home."

The little beast jumps up and down on my stomach like it is a trampoline.

"I want to throw up," I insist.

"Stop thinking too much," she says as the doctor walks through the door.

He calls me by my first name and asks to see me alone. The little beast becomes so violent that I think I'm going to throw up on his feet. When we reach the end of a long corridor, he invites me to come into his office and sit down, but I am on the defense. I don't want to talk, I just want to be left alone. He makes me explain what's wrong with me, something I feel like I've repeated dozens of times. My fear of going to class, my fear of others' stares, feeling less than others, less interesting, less pretty, and less funny.

He listens to me talk, and unlike the previous child psychiatrist, he also talks. He tries to understand and asks me questions, some of which bother me: Do I have a boyfriend? Would I like to have one? *What does it matter to him?* I see my reflection in the window behind him and I don't like what I see. My purple sweatshirt, my jeans, my boots, my hair tied up. I'm a common, boring girl. The other girls in high school are all well dressed; they are beautiful, and interesting. I'm not.

"Are you happy, Maëva?"

"There are people worse off than me," I answer. "There are people out on the streets and who are starving to death... I have everything I need."

"But are you happy?" he persists.

I don't know what to say, I've never really thought about it. So I tell him yes, so that he will leave me alone.

"You know, Maëva, people like you, if we do nothing to treat them, they end up alone at home in the dark, and they don't come out anymore."

*

That sentence lodges itself somewhere in the back of my mind. A few weeks later, my parents, my brother, and I leave for Paris on a trip we planned over a year ago. When I first learned about the trip, I was so excited. Paris for the first time! I imagined myself walking through the streets, taking pictures, and going home with my head full of amazing memories. But with everything that's happened, I'm not so enthusiastic anymore and I'm very apprehensive. I had no way of knowing that the little beast would be part of this trip. Since it has settled inside of me, it seems to feel good and it has no desire to leave. It leaves me no peace, it's there all the time, and it plans to visit the capital of France, too.

And this is exactly what happens. While I should have had a good weekend, I spend forty-eight awful hours there. As always, I have no logical reason to feel bad, but the little beast is having a great time making my life miserable. The only night we spend in Paris is horrible. I toss and turn in my bed and all I can think about is staying under the blanket because the next day seems impossible for me to face. Despite all of the beautiful things we see and visit, the only memory I keep of this trip is my unbearable anxiety.

Ever since my appointment with the psychologist, I am more anxious than before. I had tried to put on a brave face when the psychologist told me that I would end up alone and in the dark if I am not hospitalized, but now I'm really scared. I don't want to be alone in my room in the dark. And yet, I have a strong feeling that this is what will eventually happen to me. I do correspondence courses by myself, I have now stopped seeing my friends on Tuesday afternoons, and my usual Wednesday morning shopping trips with my mother are also increasingly hard for me.

6

Last Attempts.

December, 2009.

It has been almost three months since the little beast settled into my life. I have managed to find some peace by doing my school work at home where I don't have to fight the little beast or my parents. Like every year, we celebrate Christmas at my grandparents' house in Grenoble. The gifts have been opened, the house has regained its calm after the excitement of the holidays, but my inner storm is coming soon.

My parents tell me that I'm going to have to go back to school after the February holidays, but I don't really pay attention to what they say. It seems totally inconceivable to me to set foot in high school again. But as the weeks go by, what I thought was just a threat is actually being carried out. I feel like my nightmare is starting again, or rather, like it has never stopped.

This Monday morning, the little beast wakes up when we park in front of the infirmary. I know I'm going to have to fight again. My mother kindly asks me to come and join the nurse, and I immediately start crying. I don't have the strength to do what we did for weeks at the beginning of the year. The little beast is furious and it's only a matter of time before my mother is furious, too. I plug my ears and put my head between my knees. I want to die so that I won't bother anyone anymore and especially so that I won't feel this little raging beast inside of me.

When the car door opens, my homeroom teacher is standing next to me. I look at my mother, my teacher, then my mother again. And then I understand. She has asked him to come. This time, I'm terribly angry with her. I feel betrayed.

"Are you coming, Maëva?" my teacher asks me, "You have class with me; we will go together."

I feel trapped and ashamed. I feel ashamed that someone sees me like this. Crying, I tell him that I'm not going with him. I can't do it. I feel the little beast tearing at my insides and I want to escape all of this. Everything is beyond me, everything is insurmountable, and nothing can get me out of the dead-end I've been stuck in for months.

*

Over the next few days, it's the same fight again and again. Each day I manage to get out of the car and reach the infirmary, where I find the nurse smiling, patiently waiting for me. For the first few days, I stay with her in her office. It is unthinkable for me to set foot in the school, and just the idea of me having to cross the school courtyard at the end of the day to take the bus home consumes all of my focus and energy. I try to tame the little beast and control it. But when the nurse suggests that I should start classes again, the little beast is unleashed and I'm unable to control it. She asks me if there is a class I would prefer to go to and when I think about it, I answer, "French class," because I really like the teacher.

After it has been arranged, I try to go back to French class with the nurse. She's so nice to me that the students who've never seen her before think she's my mother. The teacher is also extremely patient with me. I will have two hours of class with her today. Everyone is already in the room as I arrive with the nurse. I imagine all of the looks I will get when I enter the classroom, the reactions I will get when I come back after months of absence, and suddenly, I'm stuck. My teacher is standing by the doorway, facing me, and I'm hidden by the wall with the nurse by my side. Both of them beg me to go in and I can feel the inner struggle with the little beast. *I got out of the car, I went into the infirmary, and I went through the whole school to get to this door, so I can't go back now.* I don't cry, I don't panic, but I'm torn from the inside. I want to enter this classroom, but I can't. The fear of what others will think of me paralyzes me.

"I can get them out of the room if you want so that you can settle in quietly," my teacher tells me.

I hate the feeling of being controlled by the little beast and not being able to do what I want.

"Maëva," she smiles, "if you come into this room, I will sing a gospel song."

I know she would do it. She has already done it several times and we all love listening to her sing. She smiles at me, but I can't overcome the little beast. After an hour of trying to convince me to come in, the bell rings. The class should have started an hour ago, but instead, the teacher spent that hour trying to convince me to come in. The class goes out for a break and no one pays attention to me. In a surge of courage, I enter the room, sit at a desk, and get my things out with a sense of victory.

Score one for Maëva, zero for the little beast. And the French teacher sang us a gospel song.

*

I manage to get back to class while still fighting the little beast. Every morning, I beg my distant God to help me. I want to get back to a normal life and to go to school like everyone else. I don't want to be a slave to this monster! First, I start with French class, then History-Geography, Physics, and Chemistry, until I'm almost back to a normal schedule. I say 'almost' back to a normal schedule because, despite my will, there are days when the little beast takes over. When that happens, I spend my day in the infirmary, waiting for the bell to ring to end my nightmare. I'm starting to get to know the nurse well after spending so much time in her office. I really like her because she is extremely patient with me and I think the feeling is mutual. Sometimes, we eat chocolates together when she knows no one's going to come in and disturb us. My homeroom teacher is also patient with me. He often comes into the infirmary to find out how I am doing, and other times, he finds me in the media library after searching around the school for me.

By the end of the year, I have returned to all of my classes except my Italian class, which I only managed to attend for the last class of the year. As I expected, the teacher welcomes me with great enthusiasm, telling me that she is happy to see me again and that they have all missed me. I know she has good intentions, but it's because I want to go unnoticed that I've avoided her class thus far.

I end the school year on a rather positive note. I am confident about the next year and so are my parents. Unfortunately, I will have to repeat the 10th grade, although 'repeat' is not the appropriate word, as I hardly went to school all year long. I now begin my school holidays, thinking that the summer months will allow me to rest and forget about this bad time.

Like every summer holiday before, I travel to Saint-Raphaël, in the South of France, with my cousin and her grandmother. This is the time of year we look forward to the most and I can't wait to go. Except this year is different. We are no longer interested in the things we liked before and we are bored for two weeks. As for the little beast, it continues to appear for no reason. I'm hot, I have cold sweats, my stomach aches, my throat is dry and I want to throw up. I don't understand anything. It continues to gain ground in all areas of my life.

*

By the end of the summer, the little beast wakes up as if it were waking up from a long period of hibernation. Unlike me, it has regained its strength. It wakes me up at night, gives me a stomachache and makes me cry. I know that feeling. It's happening again. The psychiatrist told us that we could try a boarding school. Since the difficult part for me is going to school every day, I would only have to make the effort once a week if I attended a boarding school.

At the end of the school holidays, my parents and I visit a boarding school near my home. I don't say a word the whole way there, but I know that the little beast isn't happy.

The director, who invites us into her office, hands me a sheet of paper with numerous questions that I have to answer while she talks to my parents. Among the list, there are some questions that I don't expect, like, "What religion are you?" I don't know how to answer that. Do I have a religion? I believe in God, yes, but I never thought about whether or not I had a religion. This boarding school was a convent before it became a Catholic high school. The buildings are old and there's no way I can see myself going to school here, nor can I see myself sharing a room with four other people.

"I don't want to go to school here, I'll go back to my high school," I tell my parents on the way home.

But the time to go back to school is coming faster than I thought. Three weeks before the start of the school year, I can hardly sleep at night because the little beast keeps me awake. On the first day of school, my stomach hurts and I can't eat anything because I feel like throwing up, but this has become normal for me.

It's time to leave and I'm undecided and harassed by countless thoughts that oppress me. I barely have time to process one thought before the little beast attacks me with another one. It knows that I'm overwhelmed by the ticking clock, by my father waiting to take me to school, by my mother standing at the doorstep to say goodbye, and it takes advantage of it. I don't even have time to yell at it and say, "That's enough, you little beast, stop lying to me!" It invades me with evil thoughts and does everything it can to discourage me. It is furious and I am unable to make a decision. I'm torn between my will and the fear it causes me. My father is still waiting for me in the car and I start crying under the weight of all the oppression I feel. I instinctively move back, surprising my mother. She opens her eyes wide and understands what's coming next.

"No, no, no, no. Maëva, please!"

I cry even louder. I feel terribly guilty and ashamed of the pain I will cause my parents.

"Maëva, your dad is going to get angry; he is waiting for you."

The pressure I feel both around me and inside of me is so strong that I am no longer the one in control – it is the little beast. I cry without being able to control myself. My brother, who just woke up, tells me that I'm being ridiculous and that I'm acting like a child. In the driveway, my father opens his car door to see what I'm doing. My mother, after begging me kindly, now takes my arm to pull me to the car and it gets worse. I start crying even louder and struggling, begging her to let go. My parents are distraught. They know very well that if I miss the first day of school, the battle will be lost for the rest of the year. As for me, I don't feel anything anymore. I feel weary and empty.

The next weekend, I watch my mother pack my things for boarding school without a word. If I say that I don't want to go, it would be like refusing to get help, and I don't want to hurt my parents anymore than I already have. But deep down, I have given up. I don't want any help, it's no use. I just want to be left alone.

*

Monday morning. My suitcase is in the trunk of the car. My mother is taking me. My father has already gone to work. The little beast is not happy, and as always, it lets me know. I have a terrible stomach ache. I twist in my seat next to my mother who pretends not to notice anything and she keeps talking to me as if nothing is wrong. When we arrive in front of the boarding school, the little beast rages inside of me. It oppresses me, chokes me, and makes me feel disconnected from reality. I cry and feel unable to get out of the car as my mother becomes impatient. I don't want to disappoint her, but the little beast paralyzes me. Once again, my mother begs me to get out of the car, but nothing works. She goes in to get someone and comes back with a lady who tries to convince me to follow her into the boarding school.

"You don't have to stay," she tells me. "But at least get out of the car and come talk to the director. She's very nice, you'll see. No one will force you to stay."

Knowing that I have a choice makes me feel better. I get out of the car while the little beast reminds me that it won't let me get away so easily. It won't let me stay here. The discussion with the director goes nowhere. I'm scared when I see the look on my mother's face as we leave the school to go back to the car. I want to disappear. On the way back, neither of us talk, but the tension makes my stomach hurt even more. I feel guilty for hurting my parents, and I feel like the little beast's hopeless victim. Suddenly, my mother explodes. In tears, she screams that she doesn't know what to do, that she and dad have tried everything, and that I'm not helping them. And I start crying again.

"And Grandpa and Grandma, you know they're worried?"

I feel guilty, guilty, guilty. I cry even louder and can't stop. Once we get home, I head to my room, but my mother isn't done with me yet.

"I haven't finished!"

I cover my ears and hold myself back from screaming. I can't take it anymore, everything inside of me hurts. My mother holds my wrists to shake me.

"But stop doing that!" she yells. "Stop whining all the time. What do we have to do?"

She starts crying again and it's too much for me. I head toward the bathroom to lock myself in, but she stops me and hugs me as I struggle to get away from her. I don't want her hugs, I don't deserve them. I make everyone suffer. The tension has settled, but I know it's only for a short period of time until my father gets home from work and discovers that I'm not at the boarding school. The phone rings. My grandfather is on the phone and it's the first time I hear him so worried.

"So you didn't go?" he asks me. "And why didn't you go?"

Sitting on the edge of the bathroom tub, I look at my reflection in the mirror. When I was a child, I used to sit in the same place to practice winking. My parents have a funny video of me making faces in front of the mirror. But today, there's nothing funny about me. I'm no longer a little girl and yet I act like one.

"What should we do for you?" sighs my grandfather, helplessly. "The other day your mother was crying in the supermarket. She doesn't know what to do anymore, she's worried. What should we do? Because we don't know anymore."

My guilty feeling is back. My heart hurts. I want to rip my stomach out, find that little beast and torture it like it has been torturing me. I want to make it pay for everything it has put me through. *I don't know what to do either, Grandpa.*

When my father comes home from work, he already knows that I didn't stay at the boarding school and he's furious. It's time for lunch. I sit down without a word, and my throat feels tight. I want to disappear. Suddenly, he explodes. Angry and helpless, he lets it out and I start crying again. Overwhelmed by tears and feeling ashamed, I run to my room and hear him scream at me.

"I didn't tell you to leave the table!" I hear from behind me.

I cry so much until I can't cry anymore. I cry until I lose all my strength. I can hear him boiling in anger from the kitchen and I can hear my mother tell him, "Stop, she's cried enough today."

I feel guilty and ashamed. I'm hurting my parents, we are in an impossible situation, I worry my grandparents, I make my mother cry, and I make my father scream. I feel guilty and yet I suffer even more than they do from the torture inflicted on me by the little beast.

*

Days go by. I am full of goodwill and good intentions, but nothing helps because the little beast is stronger. Every day, I try to convince myself that I can go back to school. After all, I have always gone, so why couldn't I go anymore? But every day, when it's time to go, it's like the little beast grabs my brain and compresses it until I can't think straight. The situation is desperate. I can't see a way out and I don't want to fight anymore. The little beast decides for me and it always wins.

Correspondence courses are the backup solution again, except this time it's different. I am now sixteen years old and school is no longer compulsory. Once a week, I go to the Information and Orientation Center, a place open to anyone seeking information or advice on their studies. I go there to do tests to see if I should change my studies. But I don't know what I could do and I'm far too concerned about how I feel to think about my future. It takes up all my energy.

Out of convenience, I start the correspondence courses again, but I have this additional pressure; my parents have to pay for my courses since I am legally old enough not to be in school. Once again, my mother helps me prepare a schedule so that my working time is organized and regular. I manage to stick to it for two weeks, maybe three, but no more. I can't stay focused on my lessons. Alone, in front of my books, I get stuck when I don't understand something, and solving the problem takes twice as much effort than I can give. I feel like I'm in a transition period. I am at home, I am trying to do my courses at the CNED, but I lack motivation. My life is on a break again and I feel like I'm waiting for something without knowing what – something that will fill the huge void inside of me that the little beast has created by nibbling away at me. Sometimes I'm sad and other times I'm not. But when I'm sad, I can't find a logical reason to be sad. My life is drifting away, and yet, deep inside, I know that everything will eventually change. My mother keeps telling me that I'm not going to stay like this for the rest of my life. This feeling gets stronger and stronger as the days go by; *I can't stay like this forever, there's bound to be something that can get me out of this desperate situation.*

Reluctantly, or should I say, against the little beast's will, I decide to be hospitalized. The waiting list for the clinic that the psychologist told me about is so long that I have a year to process the idea and I really need this time to think. The little beast is not happy with the way things are going – I would even say that it is very angry to see the efforts I am making in the hopes of getting rid of it. This hospitalization, which I refused for a year, will be a springboard for a better start. I'm afraid of what's ahead, but it's my ultimate solution. Anyway, it can't be any worse than what I've been through so far.

7
Hospitalization.

Dear Madam, Sir,

In December 2009, we asked for a registration form for our 16 year old daughter, Maëva. In 2009, she was not able to attend "normal" school because of a school phobia declared one month after the beginning of the school year. She has an irrational fear of getting out of the car or taking the bus to go to school. There were a few improvements during the year and the hope of a return to a normal life, but it quickly faded at the start of the 2010 school year when she was unable to attend her first day. Given the urgency of the situation and feeling powerless, we contacted a boarding school where we went on Monday. But again, we failed, as it is impossible to reason with her to "try" the boarding school. A week after the beginning of the school year, she still couldn't go back to school.

According to the advice given by a liberal psychiatrist and then by a psychologist at the Teenage Home, we think the best solution would be the clinic. Being on site, she would no longer have the difficulty of leaving the house.

Maëva is ready to enter a specialized establishment this year, which was not the case a few months ago. We wish to react quickly so the situation does not get worse.

Thank you for contacting us as soon as possible.
   Yours Sincerely.

*

From the moment I agree to be hospitalized, the little beast goes wild. I start having nightmares or, rather, a nightmare. It is always the same one: I'm lying in my bed, it's nighttime, and as I'm peacefully sleeping, the atmosphere is suddenly filled with anxiety. I feel that something is wrong, that there is something strange in my room, like a bad presence. Suddenly, hands come out of the dark and they hold me down on my bed and push me deep into the mattress. I try to scream, to call for help, but no sound comes out except a cry of anguish. I try to break free, I cry, and I can't breathe.

When I wake up, startled from the dream, I see my mother sitting on the edge of my bed, shaking me, trying to wake me up. She tries to reassure me.

"You had a nightmare."

It's 6:00 a.m. and I don't want to go back to sleep. I get out of bed, go down to the living room and sit on the sofa, feeling distressed by the bad dream. Usually, when I have a nightmare, I just need to wake up and analyze it to realize how irrational it is. But this one is different from all the others and I'm only afraid of one thing - going back to bed and having the dream again.

*

June 14, 2011. Tuesday. I will be admitted into the clinic today.

Last night was short, but not as hectic as I expected. Full of apprehension, I finish packing my suitcase and try not to pay attention to the mixed emotions I'm feeling. The little beast tells me, *"You won't stay there, nothing obligates you to stay. Tonight, you will sleep in your bed, in your room, in your house. You are much better off at home where everything is easier."* However, for once, my reasoning takes over, and I know that I have to go. It's going to be hard, but I absolutely have to. I've reached a point where staying at home is no longer an option; I really need help to get back into real life.

Today is the day; Tuesday, June 14, 2011, and my life is about to change. Or rather, my life is about to get back to mostly normal. The plan is for me to take the local train with my dad, to get used to it, while my mom takes the car with the rest of my stuff. I'm leaving on an empty stomach, as I am too upset to eat anything. I don't say a word the whole way to the station, as I'm busy dealing with the conflict inside of me. Once on the train, I know I'm heading toward a new start, but I feel like I'm going straight to jail. During the hour that separates me from what I feel is a prison sentence, my father tries to take my mind off of it by telling me jokes. The little beast is doing everything it can to change my mind. All sorts of pictures and different scenarios of my future stay in the clinic fill my mind. My brain is working full time. If my mother were here, she'd tell me to stop pedaling that bike in my head. Except it's that little beast on the bike, not me. The ride is both too long, as it gives me too much time to think, and too short because I don't feel mentally ready.

Once we get to Grenoble Station, we ride the tram that takes us to the road at the bottom of the clinic's driveway. With my suitcase in my hand, standing at the tram stop that has the word 'Hospital' written on it, I feel as if everyone is looking at me. I feel like everyone *knows*. I want to disappear.

The Isère River flows under the bridge, surrounded by the mountains, but I can't appreciate the landscape. My stomach is in knots and the little beast is holding my brain captive. I start the climb to the clinic heading toward, what the little beast tells me, is the end of my life. I'm having a hard time moving forward. I complain that my suitcase is too heavy and my father says, with a big smile, that he would have pulled it up for me but that he doesn't like pink. His jokes help me to calm down a little. I moan again, pretend to die and lay on the ground until he takes pity on me and carries my suitcase. Relieved, I walk a little better, but my legs feel like they weigh a ton, as if they don't want to take me to my destination. My mother honks the horn behind us and stops at our level so that we can put my suitcase in the trunk and finish the few meters we have left in the car. The journey is much faster in the car and I feel my anxiety rise a notch when we park in front of a large building.

We arrive at the reception desk where my parents explain that we have come for an admission. We are asked to wait. Wait... I feel like that's all I've been doing for the last two years. Sitting in front of a glass-walled desk, we wait for the lady in charge of my file to return. I'm stressed, but for once, the little beast is in its lair and keeping quiet, so I try not to upset it. My parents look like they feel the same way I do, even though they try not to let it show.

All around us, people are passing by and getting on and off the elevator. We are in the clinic's rehabilitation building, which is divided into two areas: Functional Rehabilitation and Psychiatry. At the Psychiatry level, there are also several units: the Day Hospital, the Full-Time Unit, and the Post-Acute Unit. As for me, I am expected at the Week Hospital on the Psychiatry level, where I will live during the week, and be allowed to go back home on weekends.

When the lady returns, we take care of the administrative formalities. She asks my name, in which ward I will be hospitalized, and hands me admission papers that I sign with a trembling hand. I walk out of her office and it hits me. I realize I'm admitted and I can't go back now. I have to report to the Week Hospital.

We leave the building, walk along the parking lot and after passing through a gate, we find ourselves in a large park with high trees and little paths leading to each building. There are plastic tables and chairs everywhere placed in either the trees' shade or out in the sun.

"It's nice," my mom assures me, "you're going to be fine here."

I don't say anything, as I'm unable to see myself staying here. I feel like I'm just visiting and that I'm going back with my parents to sleep in my own bed tonight.

In the park, we ask for directions from a nice gentleman, who points at a two-story building. Under the building's covered terrace, young people are looking at me out of the corner of their eye, sitting on an outdoor table. I adopt my coldest attitude, the one I reserve for strangers. After finding the entrance, we walk past the Day Hospital on the ground floor, the Post-Acute Unit on the second floor, and arrive at the Week Hospital on the third and final floor. Suddenly, the little beast starts to protest and I'm afraid. I'm afraid of meeting people my own age, afraid I'll be talked to, afraid I'll be asked questions and afraid I'll be judged. The psychiatry ward's doors close behind us as I try to stay calm.

The unit is nothing more than a long corridor with a blue linoleum floor that matches the room doors. My parents approach the glass door in the infirmary while I stand back. It's a nurse named Françoise who opens the door. My mother explains that I'm arriving in the ward today and that we have an appointment at ten o'clock. Of course, she knew about it, the nurses were waiting for us. She grabs a bunch of numbered keys and invites us to follow her down the corridor to bring me to my room. She explains to me that I am the ninth person to arrive in the ward and that my arrival is very much anticipated since there have been no new people here for a while. I find it strange. How can people I don't know be excited to see me?

She opens the door of the first room to some old wooden furniture and bedding. The room itself lacks light and I already know that I won't be able to bear it. I tell the nurse I would like to have the sun in my room in the evening. It is because the evening is the hardest time for me, but I don't tell her that part. She tells me that she doesn't really know which side the sun shines from in the evening, but tells me that she thinks it's the other side. She then opens the door to a room on the other side, which contrasts the first one. A large window occupies half of the wall and shines light on the desk and bed. Behind the door, there is a bathroom vanity, and on the right-hand side, two huge wardrobes. This room is much better than the other one. *Well, now that we've gone around, can I go home?* Instead, I mumble, "I like this one better."

"You have the choice, so you might as well take advantage of it. It won't be the case for the next people," the nurse tells me. I don't care about the next people.

She shows me a small box at the head of the bed, explaining that it's an alarm bell and that I can call a nurse at any time of the day or night if I need to. But that doesn't reassure me.

We have an appointment with the head doctor, who is in charge of welcoming me and taking care of my official admittance. Another nurse, Caroline, joins us in the interview. Relieved that I haven't met anyone my age yet, I hurry down the stairs. I want it to go fast so I can get home quickly.

In the waiting room, I find it hard to stay sitting on my chair as my stomach twists with fear. I wish people would stop taking care of me and just leave me alone. The doctor and nurse ask to speak to me without my parents. As I sit in front of the desk, the doctor introduces herself and asks me why I'm here. I explain briefly because I know she has read my file and already knows everything. I find it exhausting to repeat the same things over and over again. I feel out of place in front of these two women who are watching me and asking me questions. I want to get this interview over with so that I can leave and go home. Up to now, it has been clear to me that I won't stay here once all the formalities have been completed. Yes, it was very clear, until the doctor asked me a question.

"How does it feel to be here, Maëva?"

Suddenly, without understanding what's happening to me, I burst into tears. It comes out suddenly, unexpectedly, and violently. I lower my head and hide my face because I hate when people see me cry. Before all of this, before this school phobia, no one but my parents had seen me cry, not even my best friends. I had never let anyone see me cry because I'm a strong person, and I told myself that no one would ever see me cry. But that was before the little beast had taken control of everything.

It feels like I'm betraying myself by crying in front of people. It's like I'm betraying the image of the strong girl I've been trying to be since I got here. I suddenly realize that today is the day I will be admitted. No, I'm not here just for a visit. And despite my firm intention to go home, I can't, because deep down I know that I don't belong there anymore. Today, I am at a turning point and I need to go in the right direction. Not the easiest direction, but the right one. I decide to take the necessary steps to be admitted into the clinic, but the little beast is desperately trying to steer me into choosing the easy way out. It whispers horrors into my ear to discourage me from staying here, "*Without your parents, you won't make it. You have to go home.*"

"I've never slept anywhere but home," I told the doctor, "except at my aunt's and grandparents' place."

She tells me that it will be very good practice for me to stay here without my parents, but I don't want to believe her. She finally brings my parents into the office and they sit next to me, one on each side. By the way my mother looks at my red eyes and the handkerchief I'm holding in my hand, I know what she's thinking: 'What have they done to my daughter?'

From this point forward, I do not hear anything I am told. I answer mechanically with a yes or no answer. When the appointment ends, the pressure rises again and the little beast wakes up more ferocious than ever. My stomach hurts and I'm trembling, despite the heat of the summer. We leave for the Week Hospital accompanied by the nurse.

I'm rediscovering the room that will be mine for a while, but I don't want to get used to the idea. I don't want to call this room "my room" and I don't want to stay here. I don't have the strength to fight the monster inside of me. My suitcase is still closed, and opening it would mean that I'm officially moving in. I look through the big window at the bamboos belonging to the neighbor's property and at the mountain. And as I look out, I don't know what to do, what to think, or what to feel. Stay here or go home? I think I still have a choice, but I don't. My parents won't take me back home with them.

I sit on the desk and wrap my arms around my knees. I'm so afraid to stay here and to sleep alone in this room. My father sits on the bed while I watch my mother open my suitcase. I start crying because of the monster roaring inside of me. I cry even more when I see two silhouettes pass by in the corridor behind the half-open door. I don't want to see anyone or be seen like this.

My mother unpacks my suitcase, packs my things away in the big wardrobe, tells me that I'm going to be fine, that my room is cute and that it was a good idea to bring a green plant to put on the desk. She says it all with a smile on her face. I know she is hiding her true feelings and that she is scared to death of leaving me in the hands of these nurses. My father tries to make jokes, but I can tell he's also nervous. I can't stop crying. The little beast thinks that, with my tears, it can keep my parents from leaving. It tells me that as long as I'm crying, they won't leave me. But my mother has finished unpacking my suitcase, everything is put away in the wardrobe, and they're on their way out. I can't move from the desk because I'm trembling with fear. My parents hug me and say goodbye, as my mother tries to hide her tears from me. When they leave through my bedroom door, my heart breaks. In the hallway, they give me one last wave before they leave and then I find myself alone. Alone in the world and alone in front of the little beast.

*

Françoise, the nurse who made me choose my room, knocks at the door and asks me how I feel and if I want something to eat. I'm anything but hungry. My tears and the little beast have emptied me of everything and I don't want anyone to see me like this. Only children cry when their parents leave and only children are afraid to sleep alone.

"The teens have been waiting for you to go and eat," says the nurse.

I'm not sure if I understood correctly. They waited for me to eat? But I haven't met anyone yet.

"They've been expecting you eagerly for weeks," she continues, "Do you feel like joining them in the cafeteria?"

No! Not at all. I shake my head. She asks me if I'd rather eat with the nurses in the living room, but I don't want to do that either. I'd rather be alone. She understands how I am feeling and she brings me a meal on a tray and closes the door behind her. I find myself, once again, alone as the taste of my tears fill my mouth. Struggling to nibble on three grains of rice from my tray, I think about the other people I don't know and how they have been waiting for me to go and eat with them. I think of how I'm going to have to meet them and it seems like an impossible task for me. Suddenly, there's a knock on my door.

"Hi! I'm Karim and this is Robin. Do you want to meet the others?"

Without thinking about it, I get up and follow them, despite the stomach-gripping fear I am feeling. In the living room, two girls are focusing on their lesson books and a boy is sitting in an armchair. Karim introduces everyone and I feel so intimidated. I want to blend into the walls. I notice, right away, that Charlotte seems to have a very strong character. After only a few minutes, I feel like I'm on her territory. They're her friends and I'd better not take them away from her. She's the one to continue the introductions when other people suddenly barge into the living room.

"That's Kylian," Charlotte says, as she takes over, "but don't kid yourself, he's gay. And this is Vladimir. He's already in love with you."

I also meet Joe and Loïc. Joe tells me all about life at the clinic; people's relationships with each other, who stays with whom, who's friends with whom. They all talk to me with ease, as if they already know me. Joe explains to me that he is here because he hates himself and, I must say, I don't really understand what he means. As for Loïc, he seems very discreet and not the kind to talk about himself. I still can't get used to the idea of sleeping here tonight, but I'm filled with relief when I realize that I am not surrounded by the lunatics I had imagined when I first heard about the psychiatry clinic.

At 1:30 p.m., commotion starts in the ward. I am told that it is time for the welcome meeting, which normally takes place on Monday, but that it has been postponed until my arrival. My new companions organize a circle with the chairs and someone volunteers to make coffee. The two nurses come out of the infirmary with a tray full of glasses and fruit juice and set it on the small table. As everyone takes their seats, a face I hadn't seen before enters the living room. Medium length hair, blue eyes, earring, nose and lip piercing. He steals all of our attention by not keeping still and by teasing everyone. I don't even know his name yet and I already know that he's going to irritate me.

A nurse suggests that everyone should introduce themselves to me, the newcomer. They all say their name again so I can memorize them and associate them with the right faces. So the new face is called Leo. Leo, who I've known for only ten minutes and who keeps getting told off by the nurses.

"Stop picking on me in front of the new girl!"

So apparently "the new girl" is my new name until someone else new comes along. When the meeting ends, I stay in the living room to talk to everyone. I learn the reasons why they are all here: school or social phobia, depression, anorexia, bulimia, autism, or schizophrenia. I glance down the hallway and I recognize two very familiar silhouettes. My parents are here to make sure everything is okay before they go home. That's just like them. Deep down inside, I knew they didn't want to leave me here and that they would never abandon me. Being distracted by the reunion and by meeting all of the youth, I had almost forgotten about this morning's episode.

Reassured that things have turned out pretty good, my parents leave feeling more peaceful. The little beast whispers that I should go back home with them, but I know that I cannot and that I must not. Because today, in this very moment, my life is taking a turn. I know that the road will be long and far from easy, but today, by staying here, I choose to fight against the little beast that has been controlling me for too long now. I accept to be in pain today so that I can get better tomorrow. Today, I choose to fight.

*

The first night, which I was dreading the most, went well. After being welcomed by my new companions, I feel confident. My room is between Karim and Leo, and Leo has told me, "If you need anything, you know where to find me." I leave the blinds open so that I can see the huge bamboos on the neighboring property, a bit of the sky, and the mountain. I am reassured that the room is not dark. Before falling asleep, I count how much time is left before going home for the weekend: 3 days and 2 nights.

Being separated from my family is still hard. During the days, in the ward, I isolate myself several times so that I can call my mother, but she reminds me that she works and that she can't stay on the phone all day. The nurses have also noticed and they spy on me. At 10:00 p.m., I have to put my phone away in the infirmary cupboard until the next day. In the beginning, I pretend not to know that and the night nurse leaves me alone. However, I am quickly reminded of that rule by the day staff and the head doctor. "The rules are the rules!"

When the weekend arrives, I am surprised that it is already time to go home. These four days have gone by faster than I expected. Very happy to not go alone, I walk to the train station with Joe, Charlotte, and Loïc. Joe even offers to wait for me on Sunday evening so that we can go back to the clinic together. My parents are reassured to know that these first days went well. I can't stop talking about the people I've met. The weekend goes by both too fast, as I don't have time to enjoy it, and too slow because I can't wait to see everyone again.

On Sunday evening, I take the train by myself without any difficulty, which surprises my mother. Back at the clinic, I still need some time to adjust again, during which the little beast has fun scaring me. So, I decide to visit Leo in his room, and the others join us as they each come back from their weekend. I'm not alone anymore.

8

A Life in Dotted Lines: Memories of the Clinic.

It's summer vacation. It's hot and the Week Hospital is organizing an outing to Lake Laffrey. As only nine out of the twenty-one rooms in the clinic are full, we leave with two minibuses and more than enough seats. I sit in the middle to get a good view of the road because I heard that the route is full of winding roads and I know I won't like it. When Leo sits down next to me, I sigh inside, knowing in advance that the journey is not going to be an easy one. The only positive thing is that he always has music with him, so at least it will help the time pass by. I mean, if he's willing to share. I like him even though he irritates me. He's a very tactile kind of guy, always hugging everybody, and I don't like that. Hugging makes me feel uncomfortable. With an earpiece in one ear, I doze off a little until Leo shakes me awake and complains that I fell asleep on him.

When we reach our destination, we get off the minibus and eat lunch in the trees' shade, while sitting in front of the lake surrounded by the mountains. It's so beautiful. A little further, near a wooden pier that stretches over the water, two pedal boats are tied up and ready to be used. I hear the nurses say that we will be able to use them after we have finished eating. We lay beach towels on the grass and small groups are formed with the nurses on one side and us on the other. We are handed plastic plates with chicken and salad, which are not appetizing. With my camera and mobile phone, I film and take pictures. Everybody moans because they don't want to be on camera, but I ignore them.

After the meal, some of us head to the pedal boats while others prefer to stay in the shade or don't want to put on a bathing suit. As we approach the lake, we put on an orange life jacket. I sit at the front of the pedal boat so that I can dip my feet in the water. Leo and Loïc sit down to pedal, Kylian gets in the back and Charlotte sits next to me. She still intimidates me. I pay attention to everything I say when I'm with her because I'm always afraid that she might misunderstand what I mean and get upset with me. The boys pedal us into the middle of the lake and I feel so little surrounded by the mountains. Without waiting for the lifeguard, who has told us that we are not allowed to swim without him, the boys dive into the water and start splashing around like children. Charlotte and I sit in their place and start to pedal away from them as fast as we can. And of course, there's screaming, splashing and laughing. In the distance, we see a pedal boat with the nurses approaching us and we start to laugh when we see them having fun, especially the head doctor. The head doctor on a pedal boat! She's always so serious; I think it's the first time I have ever seen her smile. After several laps around the lake, we all go back to the shade for a snack and I'm glad that I'm not, like the boys, soaking wet. But of course, Leo, who got off the pedal boat, runs toward me to give me a big wet hug.

*

At his request, I wake up Leo every morning before going to have breakfast in the cafeteria. In the beginning, I would just peek my head through the door and tell him,

"Leo! Leo, get up!" Lately, I enter his room and stand in front of his bed until he gets up because I have grown tired of waiting for him. Every morning I do this and, still half asleep, he groans something, gets up, puts on his sweater, puts up his hood, and leaves his room without a word.

I like the mornings here. I like the special smell in the stairwell, the sun shining through the big window, crossing the park to the cafeteria and seeing all of the squirrels running full speed up and down the trees.

After breakfast, we settle down on the terrace just below the pavilion to enjoy the sun. This is where we meet with the young people in the PAU service. The Post-Acute Unit is a special emergency service in the Psychiatric Unit with only ten places limited to a few months' stay. The people hospitalized there arrive in great distress and are put under a 48-hour restricted protocol at which time visits and outings are forbidden. I remember the first time I met the girls from this unit, they were pretending to fight and Leo pushed them into the bushes. The result: bruises and scratches from the prickles of the bushes. Nice first impression. This is also where we meet the young people from the Day Hospital, and where I met Leo's girlfriend, a truly beautiful girl who looks very kind but with whom I feel a great tension.

It's the school holidays. There's not much planned and we're a bit bored. Mealtime is what divides our days. We spend most of our time on the terrace listening to music and laughing. The non-smokers swallow just as much smoke as the smokers. Some try smoking for fun and choke. The others pressure me to try it, but I don't give in. I've never smoked before and I'm not going to start.

Every night, at 9:30 p.m., the night nurse begins to close the doors to the terrace and we have to go back upstairs. We gather in the living room to choose a movie, close the door, turn off the lights, and settle into the worn-out red chairs. Leo sits between Charlotte and me, saying that he needs a female presence, but I don't even pay attention to his comments anymore.

When the movie is over, we all linger around before going to bed. Finally, it's time to turn in our phones. Some of us manage to hide our phones and go unnoticed while others are caught and reminded about the rules. We think we've found a way to create a diversion by returning an old cell phone to keep the real one. But the night nurse, Alphonso, isn't fooled, he just pretends not to see anything. He plays tough with us to gain respect, but those who know him well know that deep down, he is soft. If we're good to him, he's good to us. I like Alphonso.

Some nights, Leo and I spend many hours in the infirmary talking to him or, rather, listening to him talk. With his Corsican accent, he tells us such unbelievable stories that we can't tell if they're true. Then, when he looks at the clock that reads 1 a.m., he says, "Oops, hurry up and go to bed because I don't want to get in trouble tomorrow." This is Leo's favorite moment to come into my room and annoy me. And I can never manage to get him to leave. He has fun going back and forth from his room to mine, and when he doesn't come over anymore, it's only because he got caught by Alphonso.

Typically, Leo comes in to sit at my desk, sings as loud as he can, then suddenly, throws me on his shoulder like a sack of potatoes and walks through the corridors with me. He aggravates me. But I like him. So to get back at him, I annoy him when he plays his video games or when he watches a movie. I go into his room, sit on his desk in front of his computer and talk to him. Of course, he gets upset. So, he pauses his game or movie to give me a hug, knowing that it will scare me away.

*

Tonight, we have decided to see Transformers 3 at the movie theater and, for people with social phobia, it's far from an easy task. Especially for Karim. As we arrive in front of the cinema, I can see that he's not comfortable with everyone crowding around us to line up at the box office. We try to reassure him as best as we can, and Leo offers to accompany him outside for a breath of fresh air while we buy the tickets. In these moments, reality catches up with me. I remember that I'm hospitalized with school phobia and that my new friends have their own battles, too.

We buy our tickets, go up the escalators, and from upstairs we see Leo and Karim entering the cinema again. They join us upstairs, away from the crowd downstairs. But Karim, full of anxiety, doesn't feel any better and heads to the restrooms to vomit. We look for our seats in the theater while Leo stays with him for a while, trying to reassure him by saying, "If it doesn't work out, we can always leave the cinema and come back in. You're not alone. We're here." When they join us, the theater is already dark and Leo sits at the end of the row, far away from me. I feel disappointed that he didn't sit next to me.

Finally, the film is over and Karim has made it through the whole movie. We congratulate him on this small victory. We all know how difficult it is to cope with our own anxieties. On the way home, the boys are still discussing the film, but Charlotte and I didn't find it amazing. We quickly walk to the tram. The night is falling and I feel cold in my T-shirt. Leo, who hears me complaining about this, takes his sweatshirt off and gives it to me. Thanking him, I put it on and notice that it smells good.

*

For the music festival, we decide to take a tour of the city. There are concerts all over Grenoble and we plan to go to Paul Mistral park, where most of them are located. But as we arrive, it starts to rain. Leo looks at me out of the corner of his eye.

"Are you cold?" he asks me.

I nod and, without asking, he opens his XXL vest and wraps it around me. I'm strangely getting used to hugs. The boys want to go to the electro concert and Charlotte and I have to follow. Being the only two girls in the unit, we still have the advantage of being treated like princesses. The park is not always safe, especially at this time of day, but we have Loïc and Leo as bodyguards to prevent others from getting too close to us. We enjoy the atmosphere until it starts raining just enough for the DJ to have to protect his mixing table with a tarp. The music goes on, but we're not having fun anymore, so we decide to go home. The trams are crowded and since none of us want to be crammed in there, we decide to walk home. It's a long way back and Charlotte and I have sore feet. The boys carry us on their backs, Charlotte on Leo and me on Loïc. They start running across the bridge, over the Isère River. It flows rather eerily in the shadow of the night. We arrive at the clinic late, the boys out of breath and the girls laughing hysterically. When he opens the gate, Alphonso scolds us, but the incident is already forgotten when we pass through the unit doors.

*

Sunday night; I'm on my way back from the weekend with my family. On the train to Grenoble, a storm is brewing and I know that I won't have time to get to the clinic before it starts. As the train continues on, the sky gets darker and it already looks like it's night. I don't like thunderstorms and I really can't see myself walking back to the clinic on my own. I take my cell phone and send a message to Leo.

Me
Would you wait for me at the tram stop so we can walk back to the clinic together?

I've often met with Leo, Charlotte, and Loïc at the train station to walk up to the clinic together. Our trains arrive only a few minutes apart. But this time, he tells me that he's already arrived and he doesn't want to walk back down because of the bad weather. But it's precisely because of the bad weather that I'm asking him! He refuses, but I insist until he answers.

Leo
Okay, but then I want a kiss.

I sigh. If that's what it takes to get him down to the tram stop, then I will give him a kiss. When the tram arrives at the bottom of the clinic, the storm is roaring and it's raining hard. I try and look for Leo's green sweatshirt through the tram window, but I can't find it. The doors open and I get off. He isn't here. Traitor! I fuss on the inside, waiting for the tram to pull away so I can cross. When I look up, I see him standing there, under the shelter across the street. He has his hood on his head and his hands in his pockets. I instantly smile, "I thought you didn't come."

"I came for a kiss," he says as he smiles back.

Pff... He takes my suitcase and we walk back up towards the clinic. In just five minutes, I'm soaking wet and I know I'll have to change my clothes when I get there. I walk at a good, steady pace and get ahead of Leo, who doesn't seem to be in much of a hurry. I look back and he's stopped in the middle of the road as if it wasn't pouring rain outside.

"What are you doing?!" I question, as I turn towards him.

"I want my kiss," he says.

"Are you serious? Do you not notice that it's raining?" I say, incredulously.

But he insists. He wants his kiss now, or he'll stay here all night. I give up. I have no desire to negotiate in the rain. Besides, knowing him, I've lost ahead of time. I give him a kiss on the cheek and we start walking again. He grins and I roll my eyes at him.

*

Leo's been distant with everyone lately. Apparently things aren't going well with his girlfriend. He avoids us, doesn't talk to us, and stays locked in his room. It makes me feel sick. My heart aches because he treats me with the same indifference as everyone else. He spends his days in his room playing his video games and as soon as we try to see him, he kicks us out. At mealtimes, he takes his tray and sits alone at a table in the back of the cafeteria. He doesn't even touch the food on his plate and leaves quickly. Sometimes, I manage to get into his room without being kicked out. When I do, I sit on his desk and talk to him to try to take his mind off of it, but he always ends up fed up and asks me to leave. Sometimes, he carries me out on his shoulder, puts me down in the hallway and closes the door in my face. It's been four days of him locking himself in his room and four days of me trying to get him out. I've tried everything.

I've even acted as a messenger between him and his girlfriend and asked her to try to talk to him, but she seems to know him well. "He doesn't know how to talk when things aren't going well." I give up.

The day before the national holiday, July 14th, we hear music coming from The Hebert Museum in front of the clinic. Having planned ahead, we have kept a collection of authorization slips that we asked for every night of the week to use for spontaneous events such as this one. Karim, Joe, and Loïc are ready to use the slips to go see what's going on there, but Leo is still locked up in his room. When I tell the boys that I'm going to see if he wants to come with us, I know they think it's a bad idea. I knock on the door and find him, unsurprisingly, in the dark watching a movie. I tell him about our outing and ask him if he wants to come with us, expecting to get thrown out as always. But against all odds, he closes his computer, gets up and takes me in his arms. He hugs me so hard that I think I might suffocate. Then he gives me a big kiss on the cheek, puts his sweatshirt on and exits his room, leaving me as perplexed as the boys waiting in the hallway. Karim stares at me with wide eyes, but with a nod, I ask him not to say anything because I am afraid that if he does, Leo will return to locking himself in his room again.

We leave the clinic and follow the music across the road. In the museum's park, under a tent full of children, there are musicians on a small stage. The singer invites everyone to make a chain and the boys are happy to play along, even Leo. They look like giants in the midst of all of the children. Amused, I use my phone to film the boys dancing around with the children. It's hilarious. And Leo is having fun, too, after days of shutting himself away.

Around 10:30 p.m., we watch some fireworks go off. Leo stands next to me but barely looks away from his cell phone. On his phone, I see a few words he's sent to his girlfriend. 'I'm lost.'

*

The nurses have decided to take us out to the Bastille, a military fort located 264 meters above the city of Grenoble. On foot. People warned me that my legs would suffer, but I didn't believe them. Now, standing at the bottom of the mountain, I feel discouraged by the climb ahead of us.

"Come on, cheer up!" said one of the nurses. "You'll see. The view is worth it."

We start climbing at a good pace, but the higher we go, the more my legs get tired. As usual, I'm lagging behind and moaning. Leo, who is far ahead of me, decides to come back to help me. He pulls me along behind him. *Ah! Thank you.* Every time we ask the nurses how much longer until we get to the top, the same one who encouraged me down at the bottom answers, "Five minutes." He already said that an hour ago. I have decided to never walk to the Bastille again!

However, when we finally get to the top, I have to admit that it was worth the climb. The view over Grenoble is breathtaking and you can even see the clinic. While we find a patch of grass for a picnic, the head nurse arrives by car with some pizzas. When we see the pizzas, we forgive him for not climbing up like everyone else. Karim tries to convince the head nurse to let him drive back down with him.

I feel good with them. I realize that I had many preconceived ideas before I came here, but none of them were true. My mother was right when she said, "The other teens will be normal like you. Like you, they are hospitalized because they have something they are struggling with, but that doesn't mean they're crazy."

In fact, they're no crazier than I am. On the contrary, they are kind, and immediately made me feel comfortable and integrated into their group. In those moments, when I realize that it's not that bad, I think of God and I thank Him.

After the meal, the boys play a game of French Boules with surprising enthusiasm. Isn't it supposed to be an old guy's thing? A thing for older people living in the south? But, as they have already made clear to me, we're not in the south of France here. I'm often teased because of my so-called 'southern accent' and my different vocabulary...

At the end of the afternoon, we pick up our things to get ready to leave. I don't know if my legs will be able to carry me back to the clinic. This time, we take the stairs down, but it's not any better. Halfway down the stairs, my knees start to hurt and I quickly accept when Leo offers to carry me on his back. He starts running down the stairs like a madman and I'm so scared of falling that I beg him to put me down, which he only does when he really can't carry me anymore. When we finally enter the clinic gates, Karim isn't feeling well. He sits on the ground and complains that he has pain that isn't due to our sporty afternoon. I've already seen him have an anxiety attack before, but this is the first time I've seen it have such a physical toll on him. He has a hard time breathing and can't move his arms and legs. The nurses reassure us by explaining that it's a tetany attack, which affects the central and peripheral nervous systems, and that it will pass. When I see him struggle with anxiety, it reminds me, once again, of why we are all here.

*

The clinic will close for three weeks in August. The only people who will be left are those from the PAU, and some other people from various units who cannot go home or who, like me, have just arrived. However, I manage to get permission to leave as well. I want to look for a summer job and that is why the director accepts my request. But I quickly realize that I haven't taken everything into account. The little beast that hasn't shown up lately tortures my brain until I give up the idea of a job. When the head doctor finally hears that I don't have a job, she is angry with me. She thinks that I have lied to her so that I can go home for the three weeks.

On the last night before closing, the unit is pretty quiet. Leo is packing his bags and emptying his room because when he comes back, he's going to be in the Exit House, a type of shared home where people are given more independence before leaving the clinic. It makes me feel weird and sad to think that someone else is going to take his room and that I won't see him as often anymore. I think I really like him; but I don't want to admit that.

His room is a mess, and with his open suitcases and his clothes everywhere, you can't even see the floor anymore. Sitting on his desk chair, I keep him company while he empties his closet. Given the time it's taken him so far, he's going to spend all night doing it. I watch him and look for what I can take from him.

"You don't want to give me your green sweatshirt?" I say, playfully.

"Not a chance. I love it too much and it's too big for you."

Standing on a chair and nosing around in his closet, he throws everything from the shelves onto his bed, including a scarf that I later sneak into my room. He pretends that he didn't see me take it.

At 10:30 p.m., the night nurse tells us to go to bed. I go back to my room, disappointed that the evening is already over. While removing my make-up in the mirror, I see the door behind me slowly open and a head peek through.

"What do you want, Leo?" I whisper. "If the nurse sees you…"

He hurries in and closes the door behind him.

"Do you want to get killed or what?" I say in a hushed voice.

Confidently, Leo says, "I don't care. It's my last day, she won't say anything."

He takes my cushion and sits on my desk chair. I can tell he's got something on his mind. After spraying my stuffed animal with his deodorant earlier, he must be thinking of the next stupid thing he can do. As for me, I'd like to go to bed and sleep. At least that's what I tell him, but deep down I'm really glad he's here. I'm not going to see him for three weeks, and when we get back from vacation, it'll be different. He won't be in the room next door anymore. After ten minutes without talking, which is very unusual, he opens his mouth to speak.

"You know I'm not coming back after the holidays, right? I'm not going to the Exit House. I'm leaving."

I know that he's lying. His only purpose of saying this is to know how much I've grown attached to him. But I won't tell him because he has a girlfriend.

"I'm not coming back, Maëva," he insists, "I'm leaving the clinic permanently."

He gets up and puts my pillow back where it belongs.

"Good night." he says. Then, he leaves my room.

While I'm brushing my teeth, the little bike in my head starts pedaling. *What if it's true? What if he really isn't coming back?* No, that's not possible. Even the nurses told us he was going to the Exit House. I get into bed and turn off the light while the little bike pedals fast. It pedals and pedals and it won't stop! I can't separate reality from fantasy and it keeps me awake. I realize that, if Leo left the clinic permanently, I would be really sad. But that's silly, it shouldn't affect me.

He has upset me so much by trying to confuse me and tell me that he is not coming back that, out of revenge, I decide to send him a bunch of text messages. I can hear his cell phone vibrate as soon as he gets my messages, and I can hear him rummaging around in his closet, which tells me that he's not sleeping. When a trickle of light comes through my bedroom door, I think it's the nurse checking to make sure that everyone is in bed. But then someone comes in and closes the door. It's Leo. He squats down beside my bed.

"That's not true," he lets out, "I'm not leaving the clinic. I'm going to the Exit House."

Then he leaves. I'm about to grab my cell phone to tell him what I think about his lame jokes, but I can't find it. When I turn on the light, I realize that it's gone. Leo took it. I sigh and lay back down in bed with the intention of sleeping. Leo is determined to enjoy his last night because two minutes later, he comes back into my room and crouches down beside me again.

"You're too predictable," I tell him, jokingly.

"I'm too predictable?" he asks.

"Yes," I reply.

"Me, too predictable?" he lifts his brow.

"Yes!" I assert.

I turn my head away as he tries to kiss me.

"That," I say matter of factly, "was predictable, too."

Offended, he goes back to his room. I haven't forgotten that he has a girlfriend. This time, I know he won't come back and I can finally sleep. But the little bike in my head keeps pedaling.

*

I never thought I'd say this, but three weeks at home has been long and boring. I miss my friends, one in particular, and I can't wait to get back to all of them. Leo has texted me over the holidays to tell me that he has left his girlfriend. I'm not sure what to think about it, but I feel like I had something to do with it and I don't like the thought of that at all.

The clinic is a new life, a breath of fresh air. During these past two months, I feel I've changed. I realize that I can survive without my parents. It has helped me to meet people who have the same difficulties as me. That's what I needed: people who understand what I'm going through. The clinic provides a separate life, a cocoon where we have our little routine, sheltered from the outside world.

The unit reopens mid-August, and we are all so happy to see each other again. I arrive back in my room that was occupied during my absence and put my things back in their place. Sitting on my desk, I look out my window, hoping to see Leo. When I see his red car in the parking lot, my heart races so hard that my head starts to hurt. I watch him get out with his mom, grab his stuff from the trunk, and walk towards the Exit House. All morning I hoped to see him arrive in the unit, but as the day goes by, I get no news, no message, nothing. My disappointment reaches its peak. Finally, late afternoon, he knocks on my door. I'm glad to see him, but I'm upset that it took him so long to come. Later, when the whole unit comes to my room to say hello, he acts so silly that I can't stay angry at him for long. In fact, I can see how hard he is trying not to show that he's missed me. I have to text him and ask him to admit it.

Leo
Yes, I missed you.

*

Ever since I have been admitted here, I have had an appointment with the psychiatrist every week. It didn't go well with the first psychiatrist, so today I am going to see a new one. The disadvantage of having a new psychiatrist is that I have to start my story all over again. I have to explain why and how it all started; we will need to talk about my anxieties, my fears, my lack of confidence in people, and how I changed schools in third grade. I mentioned the latter during my first interview, surely without thinking that we would continuously talk about it. I sigh inside. What's the point of repeating all of this again?

"I changed schools in third grade because the lady who looked after my brother and I at the time couldn't take care of us anymore," I explain, in a dull tone, "My parents moved us to another school closer to home."

"How did you experience this change?" the new psychiatrist asks.

I used to talk about my friends from my old school with the new friends I made at my new school. For me, it was like our friendship was on a break until we got together again and picked up where we left off. I finished third grade, fourth grade, fifth grade, and then I went on to middle school. When I got to high school, in tenth grade, most of my old friends were there. I remembered everyone, their first names, their last names, and the friendships we had. But, they didn't remember me - even the ones I was once closest to. So, when I kept hearing, "You look familiar, we were in the same elementary school, right?" it felt like a slap in my face. I realized that they had moved on with their lives, but that I hadn't.

After that first day of high school, I remember coming home and finding my mother waiting for me. It was still warm outside, so we sat down on the terrace to eat a snack together. I told her about my day. She knew that I had seen "my friends from Allet" again, as I had been waiting for that day all summer.

But my joy was gone, "They don't remember me."

"If you remember them, why wouldn't they remember you?" my mom reasoned.

That was a good question. Let's just say, they didn't remember me the way I wanted them to. I wished they would have excitedly jumped up and down, hugged me, and told me stories from the past. Anything but a puzzled, "You look familiar."

How did I experience this change?

"Bad," I state, as I am reminded again of that humiliating first day of high school. This is all I have to say in response to the psychiatrist's question.

*

It's time to go back to class. I'm only a little apprehensive, which is rather good news. Before the holidays, I had agreed that I would take a few lessons with the History and Geography teachers at the clinic to get me used to attending classes again. I'm okay with this idea because they are all very caring, and I am reassured that there will only be a few of us in the class.

It's a relief to be able to go back to class. I don't have to leave the clinic property, which is one less thing I need to worry about. But I'm having trouble concentrating because all I can think about is Leo. His ex-girlfriend is in my class, so I often watch her out of the corner of my eye. I like when the French teacher asks her to read a text because she always pronounces the words perfectly. It's silly; I know we could have gotten along well together, but the situation with Leo makes it difficult.

I can't complain about my class, except about a girl named Marion, who, out of the ten of us, demands the most attention from the teacher. She complains all the time, talks about her health problems, speaks loudly, and tells everyone about her life; including the things that we don't want to know. I do my best to ignore her, but she sometimes puts my nerves to the test.

For instance, a couple of days ago, I was complaining about the computer not working and she had the nerve to say to me, "Oh, but Maëva, you're always complaining. It's annoying."

I opened my mouth in indignation before exploding with rage. I'd been holding it back since the beginning of the school year, but that was the last straw. I got up, yelled at her, put my things away and stormed out of the room. The next day, I had to go back and apologize to the teacher for my behavior.

The only difficult class for me to attend is English class. Yes, the subject itself is already a problem for me, but I don't really know why it's so hard to attend. Maybe it's because my school phobia started with this class, or maybe it's because, as a French speaker, I'm not comfortable speaking English in front of people. It doesn't help that I am in a combined class: mine, the literary class, with the scientific class joining us. There are as many people in this class as there was when I was in high school and the little beast is letting me know that it doesn't like it. After I have such a problem with this first combined class, my solution is to skip it until the two classes are taught separately. Upon observation, it becomes obvious I'm not the only one who has a problem with this type of class, and it's reassuring to know.

Even though I've managed to go back to school, it's not easy. Sometimes, in the middle of class, the little beast comes back to life. I thought it was asleep forever because it hadn't shown up for months. When the others don't feel well, they raise their hands and ask to go out, but I can't do it. The little beast prevents me from talking and I have to clench my teeth until it stops torturing me.

My school year is still difficult. Some days I go to class without any problems, but other days, it is much more difficult. It is especially hard in the mornings when I wake up and don't have the strength to do anything. But my world now revolves around Leo and the thought of seeing him motivates me to get out of bed.

Most evenings, after dinner, I sneak away without telling the others and meet him at the Hebert Museum Park. If we don't want Alphonso to ask us where we've been, we have to make it back by 9:30 p.m., before the gates close. It's because I am a minor and, in theory, I am not allowed to leave the clinic grounds without a written request. We spend evenings talking, laughing and teasing each other while sitting on a park bench. There's no one around at this time of day and we enjoy the mild late summer air. I'm starting to regain some self-confidence. And little by little, despite his lame jokes and nonsense, I find myself falling in love with him. Me, the girl who shouldn't be approached too close, is getting used to hugs. When we come back to the clinic and others ask us where we've been, we dodge the question.

But our little secret doesn't stay a secret for long. As the weeks go by, Karim starts to think I'm behaving weird. He, with whom I share everything with, feels like I'm hiding something. One night, as I leave the clinic to meet Leo, he follows me... and then he understands. We argue and don't talk for several days. He is upset that I didn't tell him anything and he is especially angry that I lied to him; but I insist that I didn't have to tell him everything about myself. But I know that I hurt him and I later apologize for having reacted foolishly.

Eventually, everyone finds out that Leo and I are together, even his ex-girlfriend, which doesn't help the uneasiness I already felt towards her. But to my great relief, it doesn't create any problems with her.

*

It's Sunday night and, in two hours, I have to take the bus to go back to the clinic. I feel terrified, even though I have already done this multiple times. *What if I don't feel well? What if I feel like throwing up on the way? I would have to ask the driver to stop and throw up on the side of the road. What would people think of me? But the driver won't even be able to stop because we're taking the highway!*

Sitting on my bed, I feel overwhelmed with anxiety and I start crying. The little beast is having fun creating more problems for me. "*You're going to be stuck on the bus for an hour. An hour is a long time when you're not feeling well, isn't it?*"

My mother doesn't know how to make me feel better. She asks me why I'm crying and what I'm thinking about, but I can't explain it to her because all the fears buzzing around in my head are irrational. I cry until it's time to leave. As my mom drives me to the bus station, I still don't feel any better. The important thing is that I get on the bus and, finally, the little beast retreats into its den again after failing to keep me captive at home.

Every Sunday night, it's the same thing. I see the clock ticking and I hear the little beast whisper numerous lies to try to scare me and make me cry. But tonight, even after I'm on the bus and on the way to Grenoble, I feel like the little beast is not done with me yet. I take a deep breath to try to control my heart rate and I close my eyes to try to think about something else. Suddenly, I get a text message from Leo. He spends most of his weekends at the Exit House and I always go to see him as soon as I get to the clinic.

Leo
Are you on the bus?

Me
Yes, but I don't feel good.

I don't need to explain more. I know that he understands what I mean. Feeling the little beast rumbling inside of me, I put my phone in my bag and close my eyes again, hoping that the journey will go by faster. These sixty minutes seem like the longest minutes of my life. The little beast goes wild and invades every part of my body and thoughts. I grit my teeth and suffer in silence.

When the bus finally arrives at its destination, I rush to get out and fight back my tears. I don't want to start crying in front of strangers. After I pick up my suitcase, I make my way through the crowd and recognize a familiar green sweatshirt. Standing under the bus stop's shelter, with his hood over his head, Leo draws on his cigarette one last time before smashing it on the ground and coming to take me in his arms. This time, I burst into tears. *You little beast, when are you going to leave me alone?*

*

The little beast wakes up in the middle of my History and Geography class. *Oh no.* It takes the time to yawn and stretch to let me know that it's in shape today. Then, it violently attacks me. It starts by making my stomach hurt, twisting it with malicious pleasure. When it comes up to my chest, I feel like I'm going to suffocate. I don't give it time to attack my thoughts, as I quickly raise my hand.

"Sir, can I do a return unit please?" A 'return unit' is when a student leaves before the end of the course.

The teacher agrees. I quickly put my stuff in my bag and speed across the hallway to get out into the park. I'm supposed to go straight back to the Week Hospital to inform the nurses that I'm not feeling well, and then one of my referrals is supposed to take some time to talk to me. But I don't feel like talking. What I am feeling right now is unbearable and I can't put it into words.

Amid the growing discomfort, I sit down on one of the plastic chairs in the grass, drop my backpack and start crying. I see a black hole. A huge black hole that is ready to suck me in, and I hear the little beast say, "*See, this is your future.*" I'm so overwhelmed with anxiety that I can't breathe properly. I grab my phone and call my mom.

"Mom! I can't take it anymore, I'm tired of being anxious all the time, I-"

"Maëva, calm down. Where are you? Aren't you in class?"

"I left the class. I had an anxiety attack." I say, as I try to steady my breathing.

"Calm down, stop crying. You're not going to stay like this all your life."

"But that's just it, Mom, you don't understand. When I think about my future, I can't see anything. There is just a black hole!"

9

Heartbreak.

October, 2012.

For months, the psychiatrist and I talked about what I would like to do for my senior year. Should I stay at the clinic for another year or live at home again and attend a normal high school? Upon her suggestion, I made a list of pros and cons. Advantages of staying at the clinic: I already know the environment and the people, I only have to leave the house to go to the clinic once a week, and Leo is there. Disadvantages: feeling infantilized by the nurses and hearing their constant, "if you're here, it's for a reason." On the one hand, I think that I could end my hospitalization since I've managed to go back to school. However, the thought of being home again, going back to school... I just didn't feel like I could do it. So, I decided to finish school here at the Care and Studies Unit in the hospital.

During the summer holidays, Leo came to Saint Raphael, a city near the sea in the south of France, to join with my parents, my brother and me. And even though a vacation at the seaside is supposed to be a relaxing time, I could tell that he was struggling. Out of his comfort zone and far from home, he had to face his own little beast. We walked along the beach at nightfall and visited the night market hand in hand. I was happy to show him the place where I've spent all my summers since I was little. In the end, he was glad he came.

Now senior year has begun and I am back at the clinic. I find the same people in my 12th grade class and, overall, nothing has really changed except that Leo has left the clinic and entered a general high school.

Leo and I have been together for a year now and everything was going well until he started his senior year at the local high school. For a month now, he hasn't sent me any messages, he barely answers mine, and the more days that go by, the more distant he becomes. He takes driving lessons only a quarter mile from the clinic, but he never comes to see me because he says that he doesn't have the time. But he has to walk past the clinic gate to get there, so his excuse doesn't make sense. So tonight, I decide to sit and wait for him in front of the entrance to talk with him. I have been suffering from this situation with Leo for too long.

It's 5 o'clock when he comes up the street. He smiles as he gets closer to me and sits down beside me as if nothing has happened. But I know him too well; his smile is just a facade. I make every effort not to cry when I ask him what's going on. Why is he distant, why is he avoiding me? But he shuts down and for the next forty-five minutes, he doesn't say a single word. I want to shake him until he talks to me, so that he can explain. But that's Leo. He won't talk when he's not feeling well. Finally, without a word, he gets up. I start to panic. Hoping to get a reaction from him, I blurt out, "Leo, if you leave, it's over."

He takes his bag, walks down the street and leaves without looking back.

*

He's lost. He knows he loves me, but he's confused about himself and about us. His new life in the high school outside the clinic is upsetting him, as he has always felt that he missed out on a normal adolescence. And also, it's Leo; as soon as something goes wrong, he locks himself into his legendary silence and there's nothing you can do about it. His behavior was already complicated to deal with when he was still at the clinic, so now that we don't see each other anymore, it's much worse. He ignores my calls. I harass him with messages, desperately hoping that he will answer me, but he never does. I am left feeling hopeless.

Both the little beast and the situation with Leo make the next three months the most painful months of my life. I lose weight from not eating anything, I cry at night, I cry during the day, and I can't go to school or concentrate on anything. I curse Leo's new high school and his normal life with his normal friends, while I'm still here. So that's it? Now that he's on the outside, nothing matters? Has he forgotten what we went through here, that we went through the same things?

We keep in touch, in spite of everything, and our discussions seem like a long break-up that lasts for months. I ask him to come and get his things that I still have and don't want to keep, but it's really just an excuse to see him. He came, twice, as if nothing had happened. We even spent an afternoon together with the other people in the clinic, ignoring each other, but still secretly glancing over at each other. He left early that day and told me, "It's easier when I don't see you." That's typical Leo: the less I see you, the less I miss you.

These explanations lasted for three long, endless months until the day he confessed to me that he had a relationship with another girl. It made me feel sick. I spent a whole day crying in my bed and hating him, and the idea of him having a relationship with another girl haunted my dreams. I hate him, but yet I'm still in love with him.

One night, I convince him to come over so we can talk face to face. I can not stand torturing myself anymore. I insist that he comes here, as I haven't eaten anything for three days and I don't have the strength to go anywhere. He arrives at nightfall and, in the rain, we walk to the museum park. Standing there, under the shelter of the little kiosk, neither of us wants to remember the good memories we had here. As always, he locks himself in his silence. His eyes are on his feet and he doesn't even look at me. I explode. I yell at him and tell him that the situation makes me sick - this girl I wish I'd never heard of, his indifference - everything. Suddenly, he comes out of his inertia. He raises his head, grabs me by the sleeve and hugs me. The moment I open my mouth to tell him that it's too easy to just hug me and that it's not going to solve the problem, he bursts into tears. It's the first time since I've known him that I have seen him cry. He tells me that he feels bad, that he loves me and that he never meant to hurt me. But it's too late, my heart is definitely broken and so is our relationship.

*

For the first time in four years, I start to take anti-anxiety medication; Xanax. It's something I've always refused to do for fear of being trapped in my body and no longer having control of myself. But it's the only solution the psychiatrist has given me to overcome my extreme anxiety. I can't say that it helps me a lot, but I have to admit that it doesn't hurt me either. Typically, after an hour, I feel the tiredness creep in. It's a foggy tiredness and it's different from the one I know, and I go to bed and have a good night's sleep.

One of the girls here told me that even the strongest drugs don't take away the anxiety, but that they only stop it from manifesting. And she's right, because when I take that anti-anxiety medication, I feel like I am putting a lid on the little beast. It feels good and my body rests for a few hours, but eventually it comes back. The psychiatrist tells me, "Anxiety attacks are for life. You have to learn how to live with them." Hearing this is horrible; we will never be able to get rid of it completely? But, it's true, the little beast always comes back. Sometimes I just don't have the strength to face it so I take the medication to anesthetize the little beast when I want it to leave me alone.

I've often wondered how I got to this point. How did I, Maëva, who hasn't experienced anything terrible in her life and who had everything necessary to be happy, end up here, in a psychiatry clinic? When I was little and drove past the high school, I used to look at the students and try to imagine what kind of person I would be when I was their age. Would I get my high school diploma, a bunch of friends to laugh with, a boyfriend?

I wish I had several lives to be several people. I would dedicate my life to something. Dance, music, art... something that would give meaning to my existence, that would make me belong to a group of people. But I love everything. I like dancing, drawing and writing, without having a special talent for any of them. And because I also like all styles of clothing, nothing really defines me. It's like I'm a mix of many people. I don't even know who I am. I once had a conversation with the girls at the clinic about the first impression we had of each other. The first impression they had of me was a girl who was too beautiful and sure of herself. Yet, I still feel like I am not enough. Not pretty enough, not funny enough, not well dressed enough. The self-confident girl on the outside is far from confident on the inside.

When I look down the Week Hospital's long corridor, I realise how I fell so quickly into nothingness and I lost control of my own life so fast. I see my daily life as a number of barriers to overcome and, the more time passes, the more these barriers seem impossible to overcome. After two years of hospitalization for school phobia, I find myself with a mountain of fears that I didn't have before. I'm afraid of vomiting. I'm afraid to take the bus home. I'm afraid of having a panic attack in the city and of what people might think of me. I'm afraid of driving since I had an anxiety attack in the car last time. I'm afraid of being sick. I'm afraid of being invited to eat at people's houses. How can I have a normal life with all of these fears? And then there is the graduation exam at the end of the year, my driver's license test coming up... I'm already terrified of the little things in life and now I have to deal with that? Sometimes, I'd like to start my life all over again, become a baby again and start all over. Without all this anguish, without all this suffering. I can't stand the little beast that acts like an infernal tormentor. I'm tired of living. I'm tired of fighting my anguish.

*

Sometimes I miss Leo a lot, other times I miss him less. When I miss him a lot, I write so that I don't message him and get back into a doomed relationship. Sometimes I think it's better this way and other times it breaks my heart. I thought it would be easier and that I would just have to occupy my mind and stay busy to forget about him. It works sometimes. But there are always empty moments, and in those moments I find that old shell that I've used as a barrier to protect myself for a long time. I wish I could be stronger than that and be reasonable and move on. I wish I could forget about him. The hardest thing was admitting that things had gone wrong and that there was nothing left but the memories. I still had my dreams as a little girl who wanted to fall in love and love only one person for her whole life. I clung onto this idea until I realized that I had to put an end to it if I was going to move on. I wish that time would go by faster, that the wounds of this break-up would heal and that I wouldn't feel the heartache anymore. Even when I don't think about it, it's there in the back of my mind, and Leo's absence overwhelms me and suffocates me. And if there's one thing I think is unfair, it's that I keep crying when he's no longer there to dry my tears.

10

The Miracle!

The movie we've decided to watch tonight has barely started when I suddenly feel the little beast waking up. It's been a while since it has shown up in the evening and this time it is much more ferocious than usual. I didn't even think that it was possible to be this bad. It's like it's been holding back from showing me what it's really capable of until now. In a split second, I feel like I am confronted with the reality of my life: nothing has changed since the very first anxiety attack I had on that Monday morning in October 2009. My environment is changing, circumstances are changing, but things inside of me are still the same. Tonight, the little beast is so violent that I don't know what to do to stop it. My heart starts beating much faster than it should. My head starts to hurt and I start to break out in a cold sweat. I get out of my chair and knock on the glass door of the infirmary. I want it to stop. I want to take some anti-anxiety medication, the whole box if I have to; it doesn't matter as long as it stops, as long as it silences the little beast. I am overwhelmed and it suffocates me. I feel like I don't know myself anymore, as if I'm losing control of my own body. The nurses ask me to wait because they're in a meeting. But don't they understand? I can't wait, I'm really not feeling well! The little beast is taking over my whole body.

I feel a ball of anxiety pressing on my stomach and it makes me want to vomit. It's unbearable. I immediately grab my phone to call my mother.

"Mom, it's me," I gasp, holding back tears. "No, it's not okay. I don't feel well. I'm sick of it, it's always the same, it's never going to stop."

In despair, I start crying.

"I don't want to live like this all my life, it's too hard to fight all the time. I'm tired."

"But, Maëva, you can't be tired at 18…"

"Yes I can," I say in defeat, "I'm tired of living, Mom."

We were on the phone for over an hour, and for the first time, since the little beast came into my life, talking to my mother didn't make me feel any better. It changed absolutely nothing. I can feel the little beast laughing at the situation. If my mother doesn't even know how to reassure me anymore, what can help me?

Sitting on the little table next to the door of the infirmary, I desperately wait for someone to take care of me. I feel like screaming in anguish and banging on the door so they understand what it's like. But instead, I silently suffer while the little beast takes an evil pleasure in ripping out my insides, invading me with all kinds of thoughts, and disorienting my senses to the point of making me feel like I'm going crazy. I have fallen into a well and every time I think I have reached the bottom, I fall even lower. So, it's never going to end.

Suddenly, I feel the ball of anxiety weighing on my stomach become light, rise up along my throat, evaporate and… nothing. The war inside of me ends. My stomach ache stops, my thoughts become clear again and I feel like myself again. As I try to understand what just happened, it becomes clear to me that I already know the answer, as if someone whispered it in my ear. I reach for my phone, sure of the answer before I even ask the question.

Me
　　Dad, did you pray for me just now?

Dad
Yes. Why?

*

A New Testament Bible has been lying on my bedside table since I came to the clinic. My father gave it to me, saying that one day I would find the time to read it. To be honest, I never wanted to. Until today. I believe, and have always believed in God. When I was little I prayed, and God answered my prayers. He also answered my father's prayers. I remember that I was very afraid of witches because of a story that was read to us every time we went to the library with my kindergarten class. It frightened me and caused me to feel fear when I went to bed. One night, my father sat on my bed, took me in his arms and prayed. From that day on, I was never afraid of witches again. But even though I believe in the existence of God and call myself a Christian, it's not the same as it was when I was little. Today, I feel like there's a wall between God and me.

In the evening, alone in my room, I start reading the New Testament Bible, which had been lying there for over a year. I discover the story of Jesus who healed the sick and freed people from evil spirits. The same Jesus who also healed my dad from depression, my uncle Toni from a stomach ulcer, and who I've been hearing about ever since I was little. My grandmother and her siblings have always told us lots of stories about what they experienced, much like the stories I read about in the New Testament. I read that Jesus came to address our sinfulness, but I have never considered myself a sinner.

For me, sin is something a bit old-fashioned, something from my grandparents' time. Yet, the more I read the New

Testament, the more concerned I become. I've lied, I've hated people who made me suffer, I've coveted, I've spoken evil. Not only am I feeling concerned, but I realize how dirty my heart is. I see that Jesus was insulted, humiliated, beaten and crucified, yet He lived a perfect life. I read that Jesus suffered in our place, my place, what we should have suffered because of our sins. And because He, who was innocent, paid the price for us who are guilty, we can, if we repent, be reconciled to God again. I realize that the gulf between me and God, the wall that separates me from Him, is my sin.

*

February, 2013

I've moved into the Exit House, which is supposed to be a good thing, but it hasn't exactly been happy because this means more autonomy and freedom before my final discharge from the clinic, and the little beast doesn't like it. It attacks me with doubts, *"You're not capable of being autonomous, you know that. You need your parents. And then the graduation exam, Maëva, seriously? You know very well you won't get it. Being stuck in a classroom for hours, can you imagine? It's not like here where you can go out anytime you want. Look, things haven't changed much since you came to the clinic and six months in the Exit House isn't going to change that."*

Every night in my new room, I continue to read the New Testament. It's quieter here in the Exit House. The Day Nurse leaves around 6:00 p.m. and Alphonso doesn't come by until midnight to make sure that everyone is asleep. I can read without being disturbed, without having to explain why I'm interested in this book. When I tell others about it, they don't understand or they laugh at me, so I decide to keep it to myself.

I am getting to know Jesus. I have been slowly opening myself up to Him since the evening I felt the little beast come out of my body when my dad prayed for me. After that, my dad told me, "Every time you feel it coming back, just say, 'Anxiety, I chase you away in the name of Jesus Christ!'" And it works every time.

The more I discover the story of Jesus, the more I am touched by who He is; by His love and compassion for people. The day I read that He died and was crucified and rose to life again three days later, a hope is born inside of me. If Jesus is alive today, then He can do something for me.

*

Jesus,
I realize there's nothing I can do to get out of the situation I'm in. I believe what I read in the Bible. I believe that you are alive today and that you can do something for me. I ask you for forgiveness for my sins and I make a decision today to stop doing those things that you don't like. Forgive me for the wicked things I have said and done, for the evil I have committed, the lies I have told for my own benefit, the people I have judged, hated, and my passion for the band that I have been obsessed with for the last five years. Forgive me for all the times I said and thought you were far away from me when you were within my reach and it was my sin that kept me from seeing you. I give you all my doubts so that you can transform them into faith, my fear of being judged by others, of the future, my present situation and all my anxieties for which I do not know the reasons. I give you my relationships, my friends from here who argue with me every time I tell them about you, the girl in the room upstairs who stomps around loudly at 7:00 a.m., and everything that

happened with Leo. I'm giving you my education and my future work so you can guide me through the choices I have to make. I give you my present and future home so that it will be filled with your presence and joy, and my whole family. I give you my money and my material goods. I give you my life so that you can use me.

Jesus, forgive me for my sins. Heal me where I need healing, deliver me from my fears and give me a new beginning.

11

A Life Beginning Again.

The sun shines through the wooden shutters of my room at the Exit House and wakes me up. It's an ordinary day, but this morning something has changed. Something has changed inside of me. It's something I haven't felt for so long that I can't remember the last time I felt it - I feel fine. It's not just like waking up in a good mood, it's more like a state of mind. I take a deep breath and realize that, ever since I asked Jesus to help me, I feel good. I remember reading his words in the New Testament, "Come to me, all who labor and are heavy laden, and I will give you rest." That's right... that tiredness I used to feel, it's gone.

Everything's different now. The sky is bluer, the trees are greener, life is different even though my physical situation hasn't changed. I'm still hospitalized at the psychiatry clinic. But something is different. Inside of me. Something is blossoming inside of me and it makes me think that anything is possible. Since what I read in the Bible is true, and since Jesus is real, then that means that anything is possible. Something is different, something is changed inside of me. I can feel it, I can almost touch it. It's like a little flame has just been lit and I can even give it a name. Hope.

As days go by, the change that has started in me continues. I feel like I'm brand new inside, rediscovering what it's like to live normally, with a hope I've never had before. This peace that I feel is brand new and it feels so good! The look in my eyes has changed, too. Before when I looked at myself in the mirror, I always had this sadness in my eyes, even on days when I wasn't particularly sad. But today, it's the opposite! There's a sparkle in my eyes that wasn't there before and it's there even on hard days.

At the end of the school year, I take my driving license test and my graduation exam, and I do them without feeling any anxiety! When the results arrive and the word "ADMITTED" is written next to my name, I realize what it means. After countless anxiety attacks, battles with my parents, battles against the little beast, a year of correspondence courses, two years in the hospital, struggling with school phobia for four years, and after everyone got used to the idea that it might not be possible... I passed my graduation exam! Me, Maëva, I HAVE MY DIPLOMA!

*

With my suitcases loaded in the trunk of the car to go home, I gaze at the Exit House and reflect on my stay at the clinic. I remember the day I was admitted like it was yesterday. The doctor's famous question, "How does it feel to be here, Maëva?" I remember the horrible feeling of being abandoned by my parents when they left, Karim and Robin introducing me to the others, Leo. So much has happened since then. There have been times when I managed to overcome and times when I was very, very low. And now, two years later, I'm signing my discharge papers. Today, Friday, July 19th, 2013, the day before my 19th birthday, I am ending my hospitalization because I no longer need it. Not only do I no longer need it, but I'm leaving with my graduation diploma and driving license in my pocket! No one would have bet on that; certainly not me.

Something has changed in my life since I chose to turn to Jesus. It's like I am being cleaned on the inside. And the more I feel this inner change, the more I want to know Him. It's different with the little beast, too. It is no longer inside of me since that evening when my father prayed for me. That ball that I felt come out of my body, that was it. It's always lurking around, trying to scare me and come back to settle down inside of me again. But every time it tries, I order it to leave in the name of Jesus and it leaves because, now, it's the one who's afraid. Now that it's no longer in me, this thing that tried to destroy me, I will not let it come back again. I don't want it in my life anymore.

*

After spending the summer at home, I am back in Grenoble again, sharing an apartment with Louise, my friend from the Exit House. A new life, a new environment. We've found an apartment in Saint Martin d'Hères. It is not far from the university campus where I will start studying Sociology with... normal stress! I don't even know when I last went to school without wanting to vomit because of the anxiety turning in my stomach. It is truly amazing to see how much I've changed. However, Louise cannot say the same. The week before school starts, she can't sleep at night. Her anxiety is nearly contagious as I accompany her to school on the first day. *No, little beast, you and I are done.* Standing in front of the school, she struggles with an inner fear that I know too well. Whatever I say or do, I know from experience that it won't change anything, so I just stand by her side until she decides to walk through the front door.

I just wish she'd get rid of her little beast. I know Jesus can heal her, too, but we end up arguing every time we talk about it. "I've had it up to here with your Jesus!" she exclaimed to me the last time we talked about it.

As for me, I am going back to school feeling normal and it's the first time in a long time that I've felt this way. Not to fight with the little beast, not to ask myself if I'm going, if I'm not going... Everything happens naturally without me asking myself any questions. However, on the first day, the teacher informs us that we're going to have to do a presentation in front of our class of fifty people. The little beast immediately jumps on the opportunity to scare me, *"You, Maëva, are going to stand in front of the class and speak in front of everyone? Remember that you were hospitalized for two years in a psychiatry clinic for a school phobia because you are afraid of how people will look at you."* But I refuse to be overwhelmed by its lies. No, I'm going to do this presentation because it's not like it used to be. *Jesus, you've helped me to get this far, please give me the strength to do this presentation.*

On the day of the presentation, I wake up analyzing how I feel. *Normal.* Louise is still asleep and I wonder if she's going to school today. She tried to go to school yesterday, but she quickly went back to the apartment after she couldn't manage to walk through the school doors. I think it was also the same day before.

In the kitchen, I make breakfast and sit down to eat, rather surprised not to feel the knot in my stomach that had become so familiar over the years. Trying all the familiar tricks, the little beast attempts to dissuade me from going to the class by, again, reminding me that I am afraid of how people will look at me and that it is the reason I was hospitalized in a psychiatry clinic for two years. It tells me that I can still choose not to go. After all, it wouldn't be the first time I'd missed a class... *No! Jesus, I want to do this presentation, I can't abandon the others I've worked with.*

On the way to the campus, I keep talking to Jesus. I ask Him to give me strength because I don't want to submit to the little beast and I don't want it to dominate my reasoning anymore.

In the classroom, I find myself surprisingly calm. My presentation partners are stressed and nervously tapping their feet, waiting for the teacher to announce who's going to go first - but not me. How is that possible? The world has been turned upside down!

"Good morning, Everyone. I'm not going to stress you any longer so we'll start with the presentations right away," the teacher announces.

Jesus, if we could go first, at least we would get it over with.

"Group Number Three, please get ready," the teacher calls our group first.

Oh, Jesus, please let me be asked only about the first part of the presentation, it's the only part that I know...

"Maëva, you'll start with the first part, Nina, you'll do the second and, Simon, you'll finish."

Yes! Thank you!

The three of us get up to go to the front of the class, where fifty pairs of eyes are on us, and especially on me, who is the first to start. I can hear the little beast rumbling in the distance, but it can't reach me. Jesus is there, right behind me. I feel His presence surrounding me as if He put a blanket on my shoulders. He is there and the little beast can't do anything to me. I start the presentation. And it's as if I've never had school phobia, as if I've never spent two years in a psychiatry clinic, as if the little beast had never been in my life.

*

One Saturday afternoon, we meet at home with family and friends. My uncle, Mario, talks about Jesus and His sacrifice on the cross, and for the first time, I really understand what he is talking about. Out of everything that he says, one thing catches my attention more than anything else. "When you recognize Jesus as your Savior," my uncle explains, "you have to talk about it. In his letter to the Romans, Paul wrote, 'If you confess with your mouth that Jesus is Lord and believe in your heart that God raised him from the dead, you will be saved.'"

I realize that I repented in my room at the Exit House, recognized and confessed my sins and made a firm decision to change my way of life, but I didn't tell others about what Jesus has done for me. And yet, I have so much to tell people about Jesus!

I have this sentence in my head for the whole afternoon and when I am finally alone in the evening, I put a voice to my heart's cry, "Jesus," I pray, "come and direct my life. I want to tell everyone what you have done for me."

So, I begin to share with my friends in university and to other people who don't know my story. Many of them say, "It's obvious, Maëva, you are better now." Yes, I'm better! Jesus healed me.

12

New Landmarks, New Foundations.

I need to get baptized. These are the words that resonate in my heart and I know it's true. I *need* to get baptized. On May 25, 2014, right before I am baptized by full immersion in water, I stand in front of some of my family and friends and five hundred people from an evangelical congregation and tell my story.

My life is really changing, I am learning so much. It amazes me that the Bible clearly says that anyone who believes, repents from sin and turns towards Jesus in faith can actually receive the Spirit of God, called the Holy Spirit. I want to, in the same way as it is written in the Bible, receive the Holy Spirit and "speak in tongues," a language that I do not know, and that I've never heard or learned. I have read about this special language in the Bible, I have heard about it in church, and because it is a promise and a gift from God, I want to receive it. So, while driving alone in my car, I speak to God and tell Him that I want to receive the Holy Spirit and that I want to "speak in tongues." I pray and, with faith, I open my mouth and begin to speak. Somehow, while speaking in this new language that I don't know, I know that I am speaking directly to God with words that surpass anything I could ever express in French, my native language. Going forward, when I don't know how to pray, I pray in tongues and I know that the Holy Spirit is interceding for me.

The little beast is no longer here. Not only is it no longer here, but it is as if it was never there. It is the Holy Spirit who has taken its place and it is the renewal that I was desperately longing for during all the years I struggled with anxiety. It is like starting my life all over again from the beginning.

Seeing the change in me, my brother, Théo, and my cousin, Maxime (who saw his mother get healed of her bipolar disorder), also repented, got baptized and decided to follow Jesus.

In his letter to the Corinthians, Paul wrote: "If anyone is in Christ, he is a new creation. The old has passed away; behold, the new has come." And this is true. Jesus did what no one else could do for me.

*

Over the next three years, for one weekend a month, I travel throughout France and Switzerland with a group of young Christians I met in the church where I was baptized. We share about how Jesus delivered us and healed us from difficult situations like addictions, depression, anorexia, and the pain of watching one's parents go through a divorce. We each speak about our own story, accompanied by a sketch, choreography, or video. We share our testimonies in churches, auditoriums, or gyms, in front of hundreds and thousands of people.

For our first performance, we are invited to Mulhouse for one of the largest Christian gatherings in France, where 2000 young adults are present. It is the first time after my baptism that I testify publicly, and as I stand on the stage, I feel joy as I realize what I am saying, "I was hospitalized in a psychiatry clinic, I was afraid of how people would look at me...". I am saying this in front of two *thousand* young people!

I spend my Tuesday afternoons at Barbara and Victor's. They are the couple in charge of the group. I help Barbara organize our weekends, draw up the staging diagrams for the sketch on which I write down everyone's entries and exits. We prepare the material; microphones, cables, stage props, CDs, and brochures of our testimonials that we offer at the end of each performance. I proofread the letters that she sends to the people who support us and put them in envelopes. I love the time we spend together. Barbara is my friend, like a sister and also like a second mom to me, and I love sharing everything with her, whether it's laughter or tears. I am so involved in this group that the association's board of directors is starting to talk about hiring me as an employee, which I am happy about.

Through our outings, God continues to change me. I have to learn to think differently because things are different. It is no longer the little beast that lives in me, it is the Spirit of God. But my behavior is still conditioned by the little beast. I am used to being anxious when I have to go to a place I don't know, I don't like the unexpected, and I really don't like going on an adventure without knowing where I will be able to eat and sleep. I'm used to feeling an inner struggle, a stomach ache, the urge to vomit, and reactions dictated by the little beast. But that was when it was living inside of me. The Holy Spirit is different. He's a gentleman, and He doesn't make me do anything, I have a choice. He's gentle and patient and He lets me go at my own pace without rushing me. He gradually explains to me that I am a new person and that, now, He wants to direct my life if I agree to let him.

*

During this time, I work part-time as an educational assistant in my old middle school. Most of the teachers I've had are still there and it's kind of fun being a colleague instead of a student. I enjoy having contact with the teenagers and whenever I doubt that I should be there, there is always something that happens to confirm that I do belong there.

Mathilde, a student in the middle school, has been having anxiety attacks ever since she started the 6th grade. I notice her struggling while her class is waiting for the teacher to come and take them to the next classroom, and I knew right away. I make arrangements with the Education Counselor, who knows about my story and who takes the situation with Mathilde very seriously. From now on, whenever Mathilde needs it, I take the time to talk with her. She is reassured by the fact that I understand her struggle and that I have experienced it myself. She is especially comforted to see that I have overcome it. We put plans in place to make her feel more at ease at school, ask the teachers to keep a close eye on her and, eventually, she overcomes it and things get back to normal.

After two years of working at the middle school, I am wondering if I should continue here for another year. The association in charge of the group of young Christians that I testify about Jesus with is seriously considering hiring me and that's what I'd like to do. I pray and say to God that if He wants me to continue to work at this middle school, He has to make it clear to me. The day the school staff comes back after summer vacation, I have my answer. The music teacher arrives wearing a T-shirt that says, "If you were waiting for a sign, this is it." It couldn't be more clear!

During the third and final year of me working at the school, the students start asking me questions. I remember that one morning, at the school gate, a student in 9th grade tells me that she has something strange to ask me.

"Is it possible that I heard you talking on the NRJ radio this morning?" she asks.

"Yes." The group had been invited to testify on the radio. It had obviously not gone unnoticed by my students.

"I knew it! I knew it was your voice," she says, excitedly, "You were talking about a group you're in, but what exactly do you do?"

I tell her about my school phobia, my anxieties, my hospitalization in the psychiatry clinic and my recovery.

Another time, while I am helping some 6th graders with their homework, one of them looks at my key ring with the group logo on it and asks, "What does 'survivor' mean?"

The teacher answers for me and explains that it is what people are called who survive natural disasters. Without having the time to say more, I suddenly find myself excitedly surrounded by a dozen students who want to know about what's happened to me. We only have five minutes left before the end of the class bell rings and I only have time to tell them the first part of the story: my school phobia.

Rushed voices race to find out more. "You were afraid of school?" "What? You went to a psychiatry clinic for two years?" "But shhh, be quiet or we're not gonna have time to hear the rest!"

Later, the same student who asked what the word survivor meant came back to hear the end of my story. I am able to explain my full story to him; that I had school phobia, that I was hospitalized for two years in a psychiatric clinic, and that Jesus healed me of my anxieties. I told him that this is why it is possible for me to work in a middle school today.

13

Free!

It's March 2016 when I come across a Youtube documentary that completely changes my understanding of the Christian life. It shows ordinary Christians praying for the sick on the streets and the sick being healed, people being freed from evil spirits, others repenting after hearing the Gospel, and people being baptized in water and filled with the Holy Spirit all in the same day. But most of all, through this documentary, I realize what baptism really is: a cleansing of sin and burying of the old life. And for me, this is completely new.

I have always heard and believed that we are and will always remain sinners - sinners saved by grace. In fact, I often fall back into the same sins and feel guilty every time, but since I assumed that we all remain sinners, I assumed that this was normal. In the Bible, I read and reread chapters 6, 7, and 8 of the Epistle to the Romans that talks about baptism, and I understand that, no, it is not normal to continue living in sin. When I was baptized, I died with Christ. The Maëva that I was before was nailed, with Jesus, to the cross so that sin no longer has any power over me, and I received a new life in Christ. So, since I died to sin, it can no longer have any power over me unless I give it permission to. This is a revelation! I soak up these three chapters of the

Bible until I dream about them at night. In my dreams, I see: "FREE FROM SIN" and this understanding frees me completely from sin. So I start to question myself. *Are there other things that I believe in that prevent me from moving forward in my life with God?*

I discover the Youtube channel of the Danish man who made the documentary. I watch him pray for people who are healed of pain and some of them walk away carrying their crutches over their shoulder. I watch him baptize people who repent and I watch him pray for people who receive the Holy Spirit. It is not the first time I have seen this, as there are well-known people in the Christian world who pray for the sick and see extraordinary healings, but this is the first time that I hear that it is not reserved for certain people who have received a special gift from God. This is the first time I hear that all born again Christians can pray for the sick, cast out demons, and baptize and that this is something that Jesus actually commanded us to do.

One after the other, I watch his videos and listen to him say things that are so different from what I am used to hearing, and I am forced to go back and look at the foundations of my faith. Why do I live my Christian life in a way that is so different from what I read in the Bible? The early Christians met in their homes and had such close relationships with one another and they shared everything with each other. They prayed for the sick and the sick were healed, they casted out demons and people were set free. They talked about Jesus, the Kingdom of God, called people to turn away from their sins, and they baptized those who repented. As for me, I only know the young people in the group that I testify with. Every Sunday morning, I sit next to people who I am only on a first-name basis. And I have never really prayed for the sick because when there is a need, it is the pastor or the elders of the church who do it. The early Christians had given up everything to follow Jesus: their family, their work. Even today, men and women still give up everything. In some countries of the world, they are even killed for their faith, but they are not afraid to keep on talking. Me too, in the beginning, I spoke about Jesus to everyone - to my friends, to my family, to new people I met. But now I try not to bother people with what I believe and I wait for them to ask me questions. When they do, I encourage them to read the Bible and I offer to take them to church with me. And why do I go to church? Why is every Sunday morning the same? Who decided to do it that way? How would we do it if we didn't have a church building? If it had to close for some reason? If we didn't have any pastors? Why am I experiencing something so different from what the early Christians experienced? When did things change?

For many months, I listen to the teachings of this Danish man, and I research on the internet, check my Bible, and pray for answers to my questions. While reading "Pagan Christianity" by Frank Viola and George Barna, which traces the history of the Church from the beginning to the present day, everything finally makes sense to me. Since the Bible says that Jesus is the same yesterday, today and forever, then so is the Holy Spirit. And if the Holy Spirit is the same, then we should experience exactly the same things as the early Christians did.

When I share my questions with those around me, some people tell me that I think too much, and others are shocked that I would dare to question centuries of Christian practice. Yet, as the months go by, I am more and more torn. Jesus asked us to make disciples and I realize that I am unable to do so. If the church I go to did not exist, I would not be able to invite people to come and listen to the pastor talk about God, and I would have to tell them about Jesus and make disciples myself.-Realizing this changes everything.

*

Imagine that you're on the earth when Jesus was. That you're actually one of his disciples. You saw all the miracles Jesus did: walking on water, feeding 5000 people with only a few loaves of bread and fish, turning water into wine. You even saw Lazarus rise from the grave. And you saw all the amazing healings. You do not doubt that Jesus is the Son of God, and especially not after you saw Him rise from the dead.

Now, imagine that just before Jesus returned to his Father, He told you - not someone else - but you, that you should go out and tell others about him, heal the sick and cast out demons. What would you do? Think about this. You are in a time when no one knows that they can be saved through Jesus. No one. But, if you go out there, you can tell them. Like Paul and a lot of the others did. Seriously, what would you do? I mean, what would your choice be? So, what would you do today? Because it's the same scenario; many people actually don't know the real Jesus of the Bible. They think they do, but they don't. Are you ready to tell them about Him? And not just tell them about Him but also to show them the power of the Holy Spirit?

Okay, let me put it a little differently: how much do you believe in Jesus? Are you willing to be made fun of because of Him? Or is it too embarrassing to tell people about Him, even though He went all the way and died for you? Would it be embarrassing to lay hands on the sick and heal them in the name of Jesus? Or would you turn Jesus' words upside down and think: what if they don't recover? What is your personal relationship with Jesus? Is He a church, a tradition? Or is He a living, powerful God? Do you trust Him? Do you trust that He will never leave you?

This is not about a church or denomination, but this is about Jesus. Not a religion, but about the Jesus of the Bible. He is the only one who loves you so much that He gave His life and suffered on the cross for you. Are you ready to no longer live for yourself? Are you ready to live your life for Jesus Christ and do what He has asked you to do? Are you willing to share the truth about Him so that others may be saved? Or are you so busy in your everyday life that you don't have time to talk about Him? Or maybe, you just want to receive things from Jesus? Receive happiness, a good job, a good spouse, or good finances? What do you think about the fact that Jesus asked us to leave everything and to go and tell other people about Him? What about the fact that He says He will provide the things you need? Are you willing to give up your own will to serve Jesus?

Look, this is a serious matter. If you don't spread the Gospel, if you don't heal the sick and cast out demons, and if you think it's not your job to do it, then whose job is it? How can there be a revival if everybody says that it's not their job to do these things or that they don't have the time or that it's too embarrassing? Come on, if you love Jesus, it's your job. Are you ready to die to yourself? To start living for Jesus? Are you ready?

Then start talking about Him, heal the sick and cast out demons. Be a witness in your daily life, wherever you are. Be a witness when you work, when you shop, wherever you meet people.

*

I've started to put this into practice. The first time is with Barbara when we visit a woman who contacted us through the group's website. She wants us to come and pray for her because she feels oppressed and hears voices telling her to hurt herself. We meet with her, and, like I have watched in the videos, I command the oppression and lies she hears to leave in the name of Jesus. She then starts to wince, spit, cough, and say, *"Damn it! Sh***! No, I won't go!"* and it is clearly not her speaking, but an evil spirit. I've already seen these things happen in Youtube videos and I've also read in the Bible about how demons manifested themselves when the disciples commanded them to leave. But it is now so much more real experiencing it myself.

One day, a girl in the group has an asthma attack. My cousin, Maxime, a friend, and I all pray for her. She can't stop coughing and she can't breathe, even after taking her medication. I put my hands on her several times to pray, and each time, she feels a little better. I continue to pray for her until the attack is completely over. Surprised, she tells us that it usually lasts much longer and that she always has trouble talking for hours afterwards. We prayed for her for five minutes and it was as if she had never had an asthma attack. But the best part is that, several months later, she tells us she hasn't had another asthma attack since.

During the weekend, while we are gathered in our group getting ready to testify in a church, we are all praying together beforehand and Léa says to me, "Maëva, I think Fleur has one leg shorter than the other."

We ask her if she does and Fleur says that she often has pain in her lower back. We ask her to sit up straight in a chair, lift her feet in front of her, and when she does this, we can see the difference in the length of her legs.

"Command the smaller leg to grow, in the name of Jesus," Léa tells me.

It can't be that easy... But I do what Léa suggests, despite my thoughts, and, amazingly, the shorter leg lines up with the other one.

Fleur opens her eyes wide, "Maëva! I can feel my leg growing!" When she stands up again, she can even feel the difference and says that she feels like she's got a brand new leg.

At the end of the weekend, a young girl who attended our last performance asks us to pray for her. She has scoliosis and one of her legs is shorter than the other. Léa, Fleur and I pray for her and see the leg, that is at least 2 centimeters shorter, grow until it lines up with the other one. It's crazy! We rush to share what has happened with the rest of the group, but they don't seem to understand what is making us so excited. But for me, things are becoming more concrete. I don't just read these things in the Bible anymore, I live them, too!

It's been a few weeks since both Fleur and the young girl experienced their amazing healing. I feel so excited, but this morning, Barbara asks me to stop praying for people like we did with the young girl, and she asks me to stop talking with the other young people about the Youtube videos I watch. Some of the young people are from churches that believe that speaking in tongues and healing is only for the time of the apostles in the Bible, and she doesn't want contrary beliefs to create tension in the group. But as for me, I am not discouraged. I've never experienced as much as I do now. And it all started when I began praying for people this way!

*

Since I started to listen to the teachings of the Danish man, the Bible has become more clear to me. But often, when I go back to church, some of my revelations become unclear and I need to go back to the Bible to understand them again. I start to recognize that the reason I continue to attend church every Sunday is that I am afraid of what people might think of me if I stopped going. But I'm not making any progress in my faith there, and my only real relationships are with the young people in the group that I see outside of the church, so I just stop going to church. Now, the only time I'm bothered is when I have to fight the guilt every time someone asks me why I don't go anymore.

One Tuesday afternoon, at Barbara and Victor's house, they want to talk about it. I tell them about my questions I've had over the last few months. I explain that it hasn't been easy to question everything, but every time I receive an answer to one of my questions, it's as if God breaks down a barrier that had previously prevented me from moving forward with Him. I have never felt so free with God as I do today!

Recently, I had dreamt of a white board with a list of things written on it. I couldn't read what it was, but I knew it was about all my false beliefs about God. At the end of each sentence, I could see the word "FREE" written beside it. But there were still a few sentences where the word "FREE" had not yet been written beside. When I woke up, I understood that this white board represented everything that God had revealed to me and all the things that I still needed to understand.

Before this meeting, Barbara and Victor already knew how I felt and about the dream because I told them about it from the very beginning. But we don't understand each other, or rather, we don't understand each other anymore. Barbara tells me that it breaks her heart to say it, but now that I no longer go to church, my employment with the association is being questioned. Being a member of a church is an essential part for the association. Now, not only is the possibility of employment being jeopardized, but also my ability to continue to witness with the group. And I like to witness, I like to tell people how Jesus healed me of my school phobia and of my anxieties.

I don't know what to think anymore. I cry so hard as I get into my car to go home that I can't even drive off right away. I have never felt so alone and misunderstood. *Jesus, what am I supposed to do? I can't go back to church just so I can continue to witness with the group. It would be hypocritical.*

Just as I come home, completely distraught, I get a message from Josué, a friend who has just returned from a three-week training school in Denmark with the Danish man from the Youtube videos.

Josué
Hi Maëva, I'm organizing my return to France and I thought I'd spend a few days with some friends in a chalet in the mountains. We'll be able to encourage each other and go out on the streets to pray for the sick. I wanted to ask Théo, Maxime and you. Would you like to come?

14

Let's Go On An Adventure!

We are on the way to a chalet located somewhere in the mountains in Albertville, France. After running errands and picking up a friend at the train station, there are too many people in the car and it is packed full with all the grocery bags. Two of the guys volunteer to hitchhike, even though Josué warns them that there aren't many people driving up the mountains to the chalet. He tells them that they may have to wait a while. But we have no other solution. Before we leave, we pray that they will meet someone who agrees to drive them. While we are praying, suddenly, two men shout something at us.

"Hey guys! I don't know if you are waiting for the bus, but there is no bus that comes by here."

"No," we explain, "we are looking for someone to take us to our chalet."

"Where is it? We'll take you there."

I've never seen such a quick answer to a prayer before!

When we get to the top of the mountain, we meet Johannes, from Germany, and Marcia, from Canada. Josué met them during the training school in Denmark. Since we're all together, everyone speaks English, and I have always struggled with the language, so I am not very comfortable talking with them.

That same evening, we share our testimonies over a candlelit meal and Josué helps by translating for us when necessary. Johannes explains that he had a huge fear of approaching people on the street to talk to them about Jesus or to offer to pray for them. So he went to the discipleship school in Denmark so that someone could show him how to do it.

As for Marcia, she had suffered with occipital neuralgia for a little over 8 years. She tells us that it is a horrible condition where the nerves, running through her scalp, become either inflamed or are somehow injured. It caused her to feel a extreme pain that prevented her from living a normal life ever since she was thirteen years old. She couldn't laugh, run, or do any activity without triggering the pain. Eventually, the pain progressed and she felt the pain nearly all of the time, even when she wasn't doing anything to trigger it, like when she was trying to fall asleep. The pain even woke her up at night. Marcia tells us that she felt the pain roughly fifty to one hundred times a day. The doctors said that she would never be healed. She went to several doctors in Canada, and even one in America to try to reduce the pain, without much success. One day, some Christians prayed for her. She started to shake, felt an intense pain shoot out of her ears, felt something leave her body, and, then, she was completely healed. After she was healed, she went through a lot of persecution. At the time, she attended a university and all of her friends there started to talk bad about her. The whole school knew of her story. They were angry at her for claiming that God healed her and for praying for the sick and casting out demons. Then, crying, she tells us how grateful she is because even though she lost her friends, who, in the end, were not truly her friends, she had God and He got her through all of it.

Even though her situation is different than mine, I can relate with her in some ways. The fact that Barbara, Victor, and I no longer understand each other, and now that my presence in the group and my future employment are being questioned, I feel so alone.

Later, Marcia says to me, "You know, Maëva, if you compromise, the persecution will stop but you will not live the way that God wants you to. God sees your brave heart; He'll fight for you. No matter what you go through, God will fight for you. Stay in Him and you'll be strong. He's proud of you in the midst of all the persecution you're going through."

And just like that, as simple as it sounds, it was what I needed to hear.

We spend the evenings laughing around the table and sharing stories from our lives. In just a few days, I make friends with everyone, and after everything that has happened in recent months, it feels good to be with people who share the same vision of the Gospel as I do.

One afternoon, we decide to go and pray for the people in the streets of Albertville. I go down to the town center with Marcia and my brother, Théo, and we ask to pray for a young man with a sore ankle. Théo places his hands on him and, in the name of Jesus, he is healed. The young man is so excited and tells us that he is also a Christian and goes to an evangelical church. Seeing what has just happened, the young man's friend, who was reluctant to talk with us when we first approached them, tells us that he has a sore knee and that he would like us to pray for him. Marcia encourages the young man who just got healed to pray like we did. He lays his hands on his friend's knee to pray and his friend takes a few steps to check if the pain is still there. Then he turns to us and looks completely shocked.

"It doesn't hurt anymore!" he says with amazement, "I swear, it doesn't hurt anymore!"

Marcia, Théo, and I are so excited to see these young men being touched by God that we jump for joy in the middle of the street, and, for the first time, I don't care what people think of me.

In the late afternoon, we meet with the rest of the group in the parking lot and everyone talks about what incredible things they experienced. Maxime, my cousin, prayed for someone who had back problems because of one leg being shorter than the other. He saw the leg grow longer until it was equal with the other. Johannes prayed for some young people with addiction problems who were delivered, and Josué and Berenice were invited to go and pray in people's homes... just like what we read in the book of Acts in the Bible!

We return to the chalet, thrilled by our afternoon, planning to end the day with a barbeque. However, a storm creeps in and prevents us from having the barbeque. We finally decide to make crepes. We just finish eating when we hear a knock on the door. We all look at each other and wonder if we really did hear a knock since it's pouring rain outside and the chalet is secluded in the mountains, miles away from town. We open the door and see a man and his wife. They tell us that they are staying in a cottage further up the mountain. They've come to get some things that they forgot in the chalet we are staying in. We invite them to stay and eat with us since there are crepes left over, and they gladly accept. We get acquainted with one another as we sit around the table and we discover that the man is a pastor! We tell them about our afternoon in the streets, the healings we have experienced and, at the end of the evening, we pray for the man's wife, Jade, who has health problems.

The next day, we decide to go to their cottage to find out how she is doing, but Jade's situation has not changed much. When we pray for her again, she explains, in French, that she has many problems stemming from her past. Then Johannes, who does not speak French, asks us, "Is she baptized?"

We all look at each other and think the same thing: she is a pastor's wife, she must be baptized! But it turns out that she was baptized as a baby, which is not a biblical baptism. Hmm, we may have found the problem. We tell her that a real and biblical baptism is done after a person has repented. We explain that, by being baptized, we are washed clean of our sins and we bury our old life. Hearing this, she is convinced. She has been thinking about it for years and now, she wants to be baptized. Surprised, her husband asks her if she wants to wait a little to be sure, but she is adamant; she wants to be baptized today. She confesses things to us that she wants to repent of, and then, with the help of Google Maps, we go down the mountain and stop at the first lake we find. There, Josué and I baptize her. Her husband, who would risk losing his pastor's position if he baptized her himself, encourages us. We are especially touched by his humility. He, a pastor, lets some young people he has known for only a day baptize his wife.

"Who would have thought that a night of eating crepes would lead to a baptism?" laughs Jade as she comes out of the water.

At this moment, I realize I've found that fire again, that passion for God and for the Gospel that I had lost. I have known Jesus for four years. I was baptized in an evangelical church where I attended worship services, youth meetings, and met the group of young people with whom I traveled with to testify about Jesus. But over the years, I'd lost my zeal for Jesus and my faith in the impossible. This zeal came back when I came across that Christian documentary on Youtube. I realized that I was freed from sin because of what Jesus did on the cross, and through the power of repentance and baptism. And today, I desire more than ever to live in holiness. Being a Christian is more than going to church every Sunday. It is about obeying Jesus and living a life of adventure without knowing where it will lead. That's the life I want to live. Even if it means losing friends because they don't agree with me, even if it means giving up my job with the association, and even if it hurts. When the association's Board of Directors asked me to make a choice between my new way of living and the position that was offered to me, I had to give an answer. It wasn't easy to tell Barbara and

Victor that I would stop witnessing with the group and that I was giving up my job at the association. But the hardest part was losing our friendship.

*

Not long after our holidays at the chalet, I attend a house church gathering that takes place once every year in Châlon-sur-Saône, where families and the young and the old meet together on a campus for a week. I am touched by their way of living as the church of Christ, which is exactly what I've longed for. During the general sessions, everyone is free to share something with the group, whether it is a testimony, a teaching, or an encouragement. This is different than what I was used to at church or even bible study groups. Here, there are "elders" who make sure that everything runs smoothly, but everyone is involved, and yet everything is done in an orderly manner. For the first time, I understand what the Bible means when it speaks of the Church as the body of Jesus.

Together, we go out into the streets to pray for people and experience many beautiful things - people being touched by God, people being healed, young people being instantly delivered from smoking, anxieties, etc. When the Gospel is preached to the people in the gathering, some are convicted of sin, repent and ask to be baptized. I participate in the baptisms and I am filled with joy to feel useful for the Kingdom of God.

Finally! I find myself in the same place I was at in the very beginning of my conversion. At that time, I had a simple and authentic faith. Today, I once again have this joy that makes me want to speak about Jesus to everyone. God answered my prayers by doing much more than I expected. I have prayed for the sick, casted out demons, baptized people in water and, through praying and laying hands on people, they were filled with the Holy Spirit. It's as if my eyes were opened and things became real. It is no longer just knowledge. Now I am also living what I read in the Bible! It is as if a veil has been lifted from my eyes. Until now, Jesus' words had been like a guide. Today, they are like a friend speaking to me. Jesus is alive, really alive.

*

My friend from the psychiatry clinic, Karim, moved into a Day Hospital shortly after my discharge from the clinic. He had not been doing well, and his situation had actually worsened. We've kept in touch, and that's why now, three years later, I have a hard time believing him when he tells me, over the phone, that he no longer has anxiety attacks.

"Do you remember the day I sent you a message to tell you that I wasn't okay?" he asks me. "You said you were going to pray for me. That day, I also prayed for my fears to go away and, since then, I've been feeling good."

He continues with enthusiasm, "I don't pretend to be fine anymore because I really am fine. I thought I was going to have to live with anxiety, you know, like the psychiatrist at the clinic told me. But it's not true; I don't struggle with it anymore. Sometimes, I get stressed out, but it's a normal stress that everyone has. I don't take anti-anxiety medication anymore. And I am praying."

At first, I think he's joking with me, because he's saying the same thing I said to everyone when I was changed. Yet, he's one of the few people who never made fun of me when I was talking about Jesus. So maybe he's not joking? When I see a picture on Facebook of him sitting in the front row of a university classroom, full of people, I think that I must be hallucinating. Karim, who couldn't even go to a movie theatre. Karim, who would always sit near the door in case he needed to get out. Karim, in the front row of a university classroom?! He wasn't joking, it's true! Today, he works at a company with more than five thousand employees; the Karim I knew before never could have done that.

Concerning my family, my mom has heard about God for many years (twenty years to be precise) from my dad, my grandmother, my uncles and my aunts, who have also experienced things with Jesus. But it was when she saw my healing that she began to wonder. She started to read the Bible and her way of thinking gradually changed. She realized that she was no longer able to do the things she knew were wrong in the eyes of God. Upon her request, my dad baptized her in our pool and she received the Holy Spirit.

Then there's my Aunt Sandrine, the one who came into my room when I was struggling with school phobia and told me to pray and that I was going to get through it. She had wanted to get baptized for years, but the people at the church she asked to baptize her told her that she had to attend their congregation for a year first. When she heard about what my brother, my cousin, and I were doing, she wanted to know more. We shared the gospel with her, which she already knew, and she had already repented many years ago. So, her husband, my Uncle Toni, baptized her in their swimming pool. A few days later, she told us that she had said to God, "Lord, you say whatever we ask in your name you will do, so I want to be baptized with the Holy Spirit."

God keeps his promises. By faith, she opened her mouth and spoke in tongues.

The book of Acts, chapter 2, verses 38 and 39 states:
Repent and be baptized every one of you in the name of Jesus Christ for the forgiveness of your sins, and you will receive the gift of the Holy Spirit. For the promise is for you

and for your children and for all who are far off, everyone whom the Lord our God calls to himself.

*

In May 2018, I leave for Canada for two weeks to attend Johannes and Marcia's wedding, my friends I met at the chalet. As I am not used to traveling, this is a big step out of my comfort zone, especially when we decide to make a road trip in Canada without knowing where we are going to sleep, or even where we are going to go. For three days we want to preach the Gospel and let God lead us; no plans.

We leave from Moncton and drive to Hopewell Rocks to see the beautiful scenery. Then one of the girls feels like we should go to Sussex. As we pass the town hospital, we decide to stop there. Since we want to preach the Gospel and pray for the sick, what better place is there to go than a hospital? But this is the first time I've ever done this!

At the reception, we ask the receptionist if we can come in and pray for people, explaining that we are not promoting any organization, but that we are simply Christians and want to obey Jesus. She tells us that it would not be a problem for her, but that she has to ask the person in charge of the visitors. In the meantime, we talk with her and offer to pray for her, which she gladly accepts. Then, with tears in her eyes, she writes on a notepad and hands us a piece of paper.

"My husband is hospitalized in the psychiatry clinic for depression at the Saint John Hospital. Please go and pray for him. The nurses know me. Tell them I sent you. I don't know if you'll be allowed to pray here, but if you've come just for me, that's already a lot."

After waiting an hour at our first stop, the person in charge of visitors greets us and says that we need a special authorization to pray here and, unfortunately, she cannot do anything for us. So, without waiting any longer, we go directly to the Saint John Hospital. But there, too, the psychiatric nurses do not let us in, even after we've explained that we have come because the receptionist at the Sussex Hospital asked us to. They call her and she confirms that she wants us to pray for her husband, but they still won't let us in. Apparently, her husband had a bad day, and in his condition, meeting people he doesn't know would not be good for him. We leave feeling disappointed that we had traveled all those miles not to see him, but we still pray for him in the hospital lobby. God is not limited by walls or distance, I, personally, know that well.

Night begins to fall when we start driving in search of a place to sleep. After driving along the coast, we stop at a motel where we are warmly welcomed by a Chinese couple. The next day, we meet in their living room to have breakfast. The woman takes care of us and prepares us as many waffles as we want. From the window overlooking the vegetable garden, we can see her husband gardening. We feel a special link with this couple. When we tell them that we are traveling to talk about Jesus, the woman smiles and points at the painting on the wall and translates the sentence written in Chinese. It is a verse from the Bible, "'Me and my house will serve the Lord.' We are also Christians."

So that was it! We talk together, share testimonies, and pray for them before we leave. We didn't do anything special, but they were so happy to host us and they wanted to bless us by giving us everything they had left over from breakfast.

Before heading back to Moncton, we make a stop in Fredericton where we meet a couple. The man has a problem with his ankle and wrist. He is completely healed when we pray for him and his wife is also very touched when we pray for her.

In total, we have traveled 584 kilometers, and for me, that's a big step forward!

*

The school year is coming to an end. I know my time working in the middle school is nearly over and I don't know what I'm going to do next. But I do know that I will not continue to work as an educational assistant.

During the summer, my brother sends me a Youtube video from the Danish man. He talks about a discipleship school that will start in September, and my brother encourages me to go. He went there for a three-week training school in the past and it was very helpful for him. But I have no desire to go to Denmark. So, I tell God, "If you want me to go to this school, you have to tell me clearly. Give me a huge sign in the sky, something obvious that will make me understand that this is what you want." A few weeks later, a friend, who signed up for this school, called me and said:

"Sis, you don't have anything else planned for the next few months. What are you going to do? Are you going to stay home while we go experience lots of things in Denmark? You know, sometimes we wait for God to give us a sign in the sky when we just have to seize the opportunities that He presents us."

There's my big sign. It's decided. At the beginning of September, I'm going to Thisted, Denmark, for a three-month training school with like-minded Christians.

I find these words written on the school's website:
"*We believe that what we read in the book of Acts, in the Bible, is still valid today. We need to return to the simplicity of discipleship as lived by the early Christians. The 'first' reformation was that of Martin Luther in the 16th century, a reformation of the Catholic Church that led to the Protestant Church, but which still today is very much like the Catholic Church and very little like what we read in the Bible. This is why we really need a reformation that goes much further, a*

reformation that deals with the doctrines, the Spirit and the whole church system. God does not live in a building, He lives in us who live with Him.

Above all, we want to go back to the basics: the Gospel. And if there is one thing with which we cannot compromise, it is this. The Gospel is not to invite Jesus into your heart, to make a prayer of repentance or just to believe that God exists. No, Jesus said that we have to follow Him and for that, we need to be born again. To be born of water and of Spirit. It is about acknowledging our sin and repenting to God, having faith in Jesus Christ and being baptized in His name, and then receiving the Holy Spirit. It is about being born again. We need to preach this and let every church of every denomination, every household and every Christian know it. Many people today go to church regularly but are not really born again and need to hear the true Gospel.

We are longing to see a reformation of the Church. May it return to the simplicity of discipleship as we read in the book of Acts, where Jesus is the head, and we are all brothers led by the Holy Spirit. The Church is not a building, it is not a meeting with a set of programs. No, it is a movement of disciples, a family, a way of life. We want to train Christians to live the life described in the book of Acts: healing the sick, casting out demons, preaching the gospel, baptizing people with water, baptizing people with the Holy Spirit... In short, making disciples!"

I know that these three months in Denmark will not only be theoretical, but very practical, and it will take me out of my comfort zone.

*

At the school, I see some of the friends I met during my trip to Canada, and I already know all of the people there from France. It's kind of nice to have everyone together in the same place. There are people from all over the world: South Africa, Holland, Israel, Belgium, Germany, and the United States. The two girls that I share a room with come from Canada and America. The first thing that strikes me is the very personal way people talk about Jesus: as a friend with whom they have just spent time with.

We have teachings on the foundations of the Gospel: repentance, water baptism, and baptism in the Holy Spirit. But also about being led by the Holy Spirit, about being a new creation in Christ, about the character of God, and the importance of living a holy and uncompromising life.

During one evening, we are praying for those in need. A woman with a headache and stomach ache comes to me and asks if I can pray for her. I then command all of the pain to go in the name of Jesus, and I ask her how she feels. She answers, quite surprised, "It's gone..." Then, another woman approaches. She tells me that she has very painful menstrual cramps and other problems that I don't understand because she speaks English, but it doesn't matter. I pray for her knowing that God knows what it is all about. In the name of Jesus, I command every evil spirit to leave her and then she bends over and starts coughing, coughing, coughing, and spitting. Eventually, she stops and she feels something leave her. That night, people are healed and delivered, and we hear many beautiful testimonies. One young woman, in particular, said that she came with a lot of questions. Over the weekend, she repents after hearing the Gospel, is baptized and receives the Holy Spirit.

"This weekend changed my life," she proclaims. "I will never be the same again, thank you."

*

Though I'm having these amazing moments, my first weeks are especially hard. I realize that I'm in Denmark for three months, and I'm struggling with my English. I always feel like I can't find my words, like I'm babbling, feeling ridiculous. Even though people say they understand me when I speak, I still feel like a loser and inferior to others. It is a feeling that I have known so well in the past and it's trying to come back. Before, I would have called my mother to reassure me and I would have wanted to go home. But I don't want to go home, nor do I need to call my mother. Instead, I entrust all of my worries to Jesus. From my experience, I know that if it's difficult, it means that my time here is going to be truly beneficial to me. The people around me are always encouraging me, including one of the girls I share a room with who, after praying for me, says:

"I think you're here to learn English and God's going to use you for that. That's why the devil is trying to intimidate you and trick you into thinking you're a loser."

Patiently, God is working in my heart. Without rushing me, He takes me out of my comfort zone to show me that I'm not the girl I used to be. I used to be afraid to travel. Now, I am in Denmark. I used to have a school phobia that started with English class. Now, I am enrolled in a three-month school where everything is in English!

So, when a Canadian woman asks me if I would share my testimony in English, live on her Facebook page, and a couple from Israel asks me the same thing, I accept the challenge even though it's hard. I know that sometimes the way God wants to free me from certain things is by facing them so that I can overcome them.

*

Everything takes me out of my comfort zone. First, English, and now, the upcoming trips. In particular, a trip based on a chapter in the Bible.

Gospel of Luke, Chapter 10:
After this the Lord appointed seventy-two others and sent them on ahead of him, two by two, into every town and place where he himself was about to go. And he said to them, "The harvest is plentiful, but the laborers are few. Therefore pray earnestly to the Lord of the harvest to send out laborers into his harvest. Go your way; behold, I am sending you out as lambs in the midst of wolves. Carry no moneybag, no knapsack, no sandals, and dgreet no one on the road. Whatever house you enter, first say, 'Peace be to this house!' And if a son of peace is there, your peace will rest upon him. But if not, it will return to you. And remain in the same house, eating and drinking what they provide, for the laborer deserves his wages. Do not go from house to house. Whenever you enter a town and they receive you, eat what is set before you. Heal the sick in it and say to them, 'The kingdom of God has come near to you.' But whenever you enter a town and they do not receive you, go into its streets and say, 'Even the dust of your town that clings to our feet we wipe off against you. Nevertheless know this, that the kingdom of God has come near.

Based on this scripture, we leave for three days without money. We leave with only a toothbrush and a sleeping bag. Several teams are going all over the country. Some on foot, others by bus or car. They leave in groups of two, three, or four. As for me, I am leaving with a group of nine people to go and visit four young people who have street evangelism on their heart. They live in Horsens, a town 2.5 hours from the school.

In the town, we spread out in the streets to go and pray for people. Joanne, Hanna and I set off in the direction of the nearest MacDonald's, knowing that there are always young people there. We approach three teenagers and ask them if they have pain.

"Yeah, well," one of them says, pointing at his knee, "I fell off my skateboard and my knee really hurts. Why?"

We explain that we're Christians and that we can pray for him if he wants. Very skeptical, he agrees. Joanne puts her hand on his knee and orders the pain to go in the name of Jesus. She asks him to check if it still hurts. With wide eyes, he looks at us while bending his knee, then turns to his friends and bursts out laughing.

"Guys, I swear, it doesn't hurt anymore!"

We take this opportunity to tell them our testimonies and to tell them about Jesus, who wants to have a personal relationship with them.

At the end of the day, we meet the others at the church where we had planned a meeting with the four young people from the *Dream Team*." Without knowing anything about the conditions of our few days of adventure, they invite us to come and eat and sleep at their home - which is a real blessing! After the meal, we break bread together in memory of what Jesus has done for us, sing and share testimonies. It was a real moment of brotherly communion.

The next day we head back to the streets to pray for people. This time, I am with Timothée, Mathias and Joanne. After spending the day praying for people and preaching the Gospel, we decide to join the others. On the way, we come across a wild apple tree and, since we haven't eaten since breakfast, Timothy starts to pick some for us and gives some to the people passing by. As for Mathias, he offers to pray for two Muslim women. One is healed of a disc problem in her back and the other is freed from a spirit of fear in the middle of the street! The two women are touched and invite us into their home to hear more about Jesus. We arrive there and get to know the children and the father and, with the help of one of their daughters, who translates from English to Turkish, Mathias explains the Gospel to them. When we pray for them, the whole family is powerfully touched by the Holy Spirit and they say that they have never felt such peace. The parents ask us to pray for their children and even insist that we stay and eat with them.

Gospel of Matthew, Chapter 6:
Therefore I tell you, do not be anxious about your life, what you will eat or what you will drink, nor about your body, what you will put on. Is not life more than food, and the body more than clothing? Look at the birds of the air: they neither sow nor reap nor gather into barns, and yet your heavenly Father feeds them. Are you not of more value than they? And which of you by being anxious can add a single hour to his span of life? And why are you anxious about clothing? Consider the lilies of the field, how they grow: they neither toil nor spin, yet I tell you, even Solomon in all his glory was not arrayed like one of these. But if God so clothes the grass of the field, which today is alive and tomorrow is thrown into the oven, will he not much more clothe you, O you of little faith? Therefore do not be anxious, saying, 'What shall we eat?' or 'What shall we drink?' or 'What shall we wear?' For the Gentiles seek after all these things, and your heavenly Father knows that you need them all. But seek first the kingdom of God and his righteousness, and all these things will be added to you. Therefore do not be anxious about tomorrow, for tomorrow will be anxious for itself. Sufficient for the day is its own trouble.

I must have read these words that Jesus spoke dozens of times in the Bible, but it is completely different to actually experience what He said. Usually, when I go somewhere, I take everything with me and anticipate the unpredictable. It was the first time that I went without any money and only a toothbrush and a sleeping bag and trusted that God would provide for me. And I didn't lack anything. We head back to the school and I ponder all the amazing things God did in just three days.

*

There's a refugee camp an hour away from the school. A small team has already visited there and met Peter, a Christian that they prayed for and who received the Holy Spirit. They decide to go back to the camp and I join them. As we walk around the camp to see if any of them need healing and would be open to the Gospel, we approach four Muslim men sitting around a table, one of whom, we discover, knows a woman who needs prayer for her knee. We find her in her house and are surprised to see the cross and images of Jesus hanging on the walls. When we lay our hands on her, she is completely healed. We also pray for her husband, Michael, an older man, who is healed of back pain. As time goes by, other people join us, and altogether, there are about a dozen people in the little room. They are all people of different nationalities and are a group of believers who meet every night to pray and praise God! We talk with them, read Bible passages about the Holy Spirit and they decide that they want to receive Him. We pray for them and they all start speaking in tongues. With tears in his eyes, Michael takes my hand and says to me, "I have him!"

I am so touched by their humble heart and their thirst for God. Among these people, I meet Ali. Ali is not a Christian. He lives in the same house as Peter, which is how some of the team met him the first time they came. They had prayed for his back, but he's still in a lot of pain, which you can see by the way he walks. We then suggest to Michael, who has been healed, to lay hands on Ali like we did when we prayed for him. Michael, his wife, and others who have just received the Holy Spirit, pray for Ali with faith, and he is healed! As Ali accompanies us to see his roommate, Peter, he doesn't stop thanking Jesus for healing him of his back pain.

Peter and Ali offer us some food and drinks and we spend the rest of the afternoon with them. Ali shows me pictures of his life in Afghanistan and of his brothers. When I ask him if he is still in contact with them, he tells me that he is not. They died in the bombing. I try to put myself in his shoes and try to imagine what it must be like to lose your family and to find yourself in a foreign country without knowing what awaits you. But I can't imagine. Looking at this man who must have suffered so much in his life, the only thing that comes to my mind is that he and all of the people here need Jesus.

We are invited to eat with this new group of believers a week later. We make our way there, and a few meters from arriving, the engine in our mini bus starts making a strange noise and breaks down. We walk the last few meters to meet the families from Iran and Afghanistan who welcome us with open arms. A festive atmosphere and happiness fill the small house as the oriental music plays in the background. While the meal is being prepared, we are introduced to the dances of their countries and we pray for one of the women who wants to receive the Holy Spirit and speak in tongues.

Another bus arrives to pick us up just as the meal is served. Earlier in the afternoon, we had called some people from the school to come and pick us up, but we didn't think they would arrive so quickly. We had to eat the delicious Iranian meal quickly, and our hosts put some of the leftovers in small boxes so that we could take some with us on our journey. It was hard to say goodbye to them. We knew that it was the last time we would see them because we were leaving for new destinations...

*

For the first destination, the whole school (about 100 people) travels to Kristiansand, Norway, for a weekend seminar. The purpose is to share the message of the Gospel and to teach born again Christians that they can, indeed, pray for the sick, cast out demons and baptize people. After the seminar, we split up into teams and scatter around the country and are welcomed into the homes of different people. With my team, we hold another seminar in Haugesund for about 50 people, where I give my testimony… in English! The seminar takes place at a second-chance school where we meet a young man who is healed after we pray for him. We preach the Gospel to him, he repents, and we baptize him later that night.

During these days, the Haugesund team is split between different families. Sophie and I stay with the daughter of a retired couple, who live only a few meters away from her. Every day, we walk over to have breakfast and dinner with the retired couple, who are hosting another part of the team. They take care of us like we are their own grandchildren. Torunn prepares Norwegian specialties for us and Kristian enthusiastically shows us around the town of Karmøy. Not only do they welcome us into their home, give us food and lodging, but Kristian gives us money like my grandfather would have done. Right before we leave, he gives us each 500kr, approximately $50, and when we refuse it, he says with a wink, "Just take it and say thank you."

We are blessed by our time with them all and touched by their hospitality and generosity. Torunn particularly touches my heart because, although she speaks very little English, she tries very hard to communicate with us.

For the last days of our trip, we travel to Grimstad, located in the east of the country. There, we stay with Thor-Egil and his family. Their house is not big enough for us, so we sleep in their camper van. We are intrigued to hear that their family's plan is to use the camper van to go on a tour of the Balkans to preach the Gospel. Together, we go out on the streets to pray for people, discover Norwegian culture and have a really great time of fellowship. What I will remember most is the love and unity I felt in each family I visited. Though I don't know them when I arrive, it is like being with my family - my family in Christ.

*

Later in the training school, the students split up on different missionary trips. I, along with four of my new friends, head off to Switzerland, the home of one of the students, Bastien. We visit the house churches he belongs to there to encourage them, and in the end, I am the one encouraged. Each group is different: one is a group of young people, another is a group of people of all ages, and another is a group of families and couples. We see that each group has its own way of functioning. The young people meet once or twice a week to eat together, sing and share a teaching. The group with people of all ages has a Bible study. And the group of families and couples have meals together before praying for each other in small groups. Church exactly the way I want to live it!

It is a time of fun and laughter. With my little team, we hike, visit people, pray for people on the streets, and also baptize a girl Bastien knows. The strongest thing for me during my stay in Switzerland is meeting Stéphanie. During one of the house church meetings, after hearing my testimony, a man tells me that I should meet his friend, Stéphanie, who has anxiety problems. When we meet, I find out that Stéphanie had prayed to God for a sign, something that would give her hope to get through her anxiety. The same day she prayed, she came across my website and, after reading my testimony, she was greatly touched. She had planned on contacting me. When her friend, the one whom I met at the house church, told her about me, she realized that I was the girl from the blog!

Now, a few days later, we arrive at her place to eat together. It is like visiting a good friend, even though we don't know each other. She tells us that her anxiety started years ago and that after smoking some marijuana, she felt evil spirits come into her. We share the Gospel with her and she tells us that she had already repented and was baptized. We then pray for her and encourage her to renew her mind with the Word of God. Stéphanie has become my friend and she continues to be one of my most beautiful encouragements.

*

With about twenty students, we embark on a missionary trip to Dubai. With Islam being the official religion, we organize seminars in houses so that we will not attract attention. We begin by doing a seminar in the house of an Indian family, which really touches me. Eighty people are present in their yard. Most of them are already baptized in water but have not yet received the Holy Spirit. We all pray together and lay hands on them. One by one, the Holy Spirit comes down upon each of them and they begin to speak in tongues, just like we read in the Bible on the day of Pentecost! It was beautiful.

Next, we hold a seminar at Rosa's home, a forty-year-old Indonesian woman who has been living in Dubai for several years with her Dutch husband and children. She has invited us into her big house, where we are able to gather about fifty people.

The first time I met her, I asked her what her job was and she answered, "I work for my father. He has the largest human resources company in the world."

I thought, wow, he must be somebody important... As the days go by and I spend more time with her, I realize that she meant that she works for God! Together, with other friends from the school, we stay at her house for another week to help her minister to people. We join her house church, meet people on the streets and visit the souks of Old Dubai. I am particularly moved by her husband's welcoming cooperation towards us all. Although he is not a Christian, he let us organize a seminar and stay in his house.

Rosa is now one of my closest friends and is a role model for me. She manages to balance her life as a wife, a mother, and as a daughter who works for the largest company in the world...

Dubai turns out to be another opportunity to step out of my comfort zone. We spend a night sleeping outside in the desert with only a mattress and a sleeping bag. It ends up as a great experience! Then, Torben, the Danish man from the Youtube videos, asks me and three other people if we want to go with him and visit a businessman who has contacted him to come and pray for his employees. At their workplace, we tell them the good news of Jesus Christ, pray for them, and, again, I share my testimony in English.

*

Throughout the three month school, God is working on my identity. The feeling of being inferior to others and feeling like a little girl chases me for weeks, until God starts to speak very clearly to me about who I am:

While looking at myself in the mirror, I hear the same gentle voice as I did that day in the psychiatry clinic right after my father had prayed for me, "*Maëva, stop thinking of yourself as a little girl. That's not what I think about you.*"

And God continues to talk to me throughout the school:

"*You are my daughter. You are no less important and no less valuable than anyone else here. Stop listening to the devil, who is trying to make you believe otherwise.*"

"*What right do you have to think, for one second, that you're ugly and that some part of your body doesn't suit you. I created you. I created you in my image and I formed you as I wanted you to be. When you criticize yourself and judge yourself, you judge me. I created you just as you are. You're beautiful, you're my princess; my beloved daughter.*"

Then, during small group meetings, Torben came to talk with our girls' group and speaks to us as a father would. And, just in case it wasn't already clear for me, Torben's words stand out, "God created you in his image. You are his beloved daughters, his princesses. Finding yourself ugly is like watching God make a perfect painting and calling it ugly. It would be great if you could look in the mirror and find yourself beautiful."

My last challenge in the three month school is when Torben asks me to share my testimony, in English, of course, on his Youtube channel, which has more than 80,000 followers. The feeling of inferiority that I felt during the first few weeks of the school comes back and I know there is only one thing to do to silence it: testify. So I did it; and that put an end to the fear I had of speaking English. Sometimes the way God wants to free us from certain things is by getting us to face them.

15

Epilogue.

Today, my life is completely different and I am still amazed at how much God has transformed me. When I talk about my school phobia, I feel like I'm telling someone else's story. Jesus has completely freed me from my fears, and now, I love doing all of the things that used to scare me, such as traveling, meeting new people, living spontaneously, and speaking English. God continues to change me and I am learning to live with Him.

At the school in Denmark, I had a dream where I was on a totally empty platform above the clouds. It represented our world. If we add houses, businesses, shopping malls, and hobbies on this platform, we add things that keep us busy and distracted. But if we take all that away, what's left? What is the meaning of our life? We were not created to pay bills, hoard material goods, and then die. When we die, we won't take our car, our phone, our money, or anything we own with us. The only thing that will be left will be God, the relationship we have with Him, and the way we have lived.

Together, with other Christians, I am now living the "church" the way I always longed for. Like the first disciples, we meet together to pray, read the Bible, eat, share testimonies and encourage each other. We pray for the sick, cast out demons and preach the Kingdom of God. We baptize those who repent and lay hands on them and pray that they will receive the Holy Spirit. I have always wanted to dedicate my life to something and now I have found the meaning of my existence. Now I want to live for the sake of the Gospel and for Jesus, who restored me.

16

How about you?

Imagine we're playing chess. You have your pawns and I have mine. I start playing and then it's your turn. Then it's mine, then yours. Now it's my turn again. Am I allowed to move as many pawns as I want until the game is over? Of course not. Because there are rules that we need to follow to play the game properly. Well, it's the same with God.

Imagine playing chess with God. God starts the game: He creates you. You play your turn: you sin. God plays again and to make up for your sin, He makes his best move: He sends Jesus Christ to take the punishment that you deserve for the sin you have committed. Now it's your turn to play. But if you don't do anything, the game will be paused because God has already played His turn and is now waiting for you to make your move.

The next move you need to make in order to continue the game is to repent. When you do that, God is faithful to move: He forgives you. When you get baptized, God sets you free and cleanses you of your sins. When you ask for it and/or are prayed for, you receive the Holy Spirit. This is the kind of game God wants to play with us. To make sure you understand, I'm going to tell you the whole story.

In the very beginning, God created Adam and Eve and placed them in a beautiful garden with everything they needed. They lived in communion with God and everything was perfect. There were no wars, no suffering, no diseases, and none of the horrible things we know in our world today. In this garden, there were two trees in particular: the tree of life and the tree of the knowledge of good and evil. God told them that they could eat the fruit from all the trees in the garden except from the tree of the knowledge of good and evil. If they eat of that tree, they would surely die. God wanted a sincere relationship with man, which is why He created a tree that they were not allowed to eat from. He wanted them to have the choice to either obey Him and thus, show that they loved Him, or disobey Him. Adam and Eve were free to eat from the tree of life and live forever, but instead, they disobeyed God by eating the fruit from the tree that God had forbidden them to eat from.

From that moment on, their relationship with God was broken. God then banned them out of the garden to keep them from eating from the tree of life and to prevent sin from becoming an eternal problem. Adam and Eve had children, who also had children, and all of them committed evil in the sight of God. Today, we live in a world of death, wars, and suffering and it is a world that no longer resembles the one that God created in the beginning.

The problem is sin, but we often don't understand sin because we always compare ourselves to those who have done worse than us. And by comparing ourselves to each other, we think that we are rather good people. But we forget that we are in a fallen world and if we would compare ourselves to God, or even to Adam and Eve before they sinned, we would have a completely different standard of comparison.

Let's take the example of lying. Jesus said that no liar will enter the kingdom of God and that they will be thrown into hell. Wow, that's radical. We would be more inclined to say, "A lie is not that bad!" But, it all depends on who we lie to. If I lie to a two-year-old, there won't be any consequences because there is nothing that the child could do to me. But if

I lie to my husband, he could divorce me. If I lie to my boss, I could get fired. And if I lie to the judge in a court of law, I could go to jail! But we're still talking about a lie. But the more authority the person has, the more severe the consequences. Jesus was very clear about this: liars will go to hell.

But Jesus does not only judge what we do. He also judges the desires of our heart. If we have hatred for someone, in His eyes, we are already a murderer. Even though we didn't kill someone physically, we are still guilty in God's eyes because we killed that person in our hearts. Jesus also said that if we look at someone who is not our husband or wife with lust, we have already committed adultery in our heart. It is important to understand that God has decreed what is right and what is wrong. Our own definition of what we think is right or wrong does not change this. If I go to England, where people drive on the left side of the road, and get stopped by the police because I'm driving on the right side, I won't be able to justify myself by saying that I come from France and that in France, we drive on the right. The policeman would tell me that while I am in England, I must respect the rules of the country. It's the same with God: He has set the rules and one day we are going to stand before Him to give an account of how we have lived our lives. And on that day, we won't be able to say: "yes, but...". He won't be interested in our excuses or our definition of right and wrong, and He will judge us by the rules He has set.

To illustrate this, imagine that there is a special phone app where I can see your whole life when I take a picture of you. I know that you have done many good things, that you have helped people, that you have given to charity, but that is not what I am looking at. Because when you find yourself in a courtroom, you're not there to talk about the good things you've done, you're there to talk about the crime you've committed. That's the only thing the judge cares about. Imagine that I put together everything bad you have ever done: not only what you have done physically, but also what you did not do, what you should have done, everything you have said, and all of your secret thoughts. I'm talking about the bad and nasty things you have done: all the lies, the cheating, the stealing, and everything you did when no one was watching you. Imagine I make a video of all of these bad things you have done and show it to all your family and friends. Would you like that? I wouldn't either! It's interesting that we wouldn't like it, even though we know that they are as guilty as we are. We would be so ashamed if our most secret thoughts and the things we did while no one was watching us were exposed for everyone to see. Personally, I would move far away so that I would never see anyone I knew ever again! However, one day, we will find ourselves in God's courtroom. He is holy, He knows everything, He sees everything, and He has never sinned. If we feel ashamed in front of other people who have sinned like us, imagine how we will feel standing before a holy, righteous God. On that day, we will not be able to say that it was someone else's fault or that we are a good person. On that day, we will know that we are guilty and that we deserve hell because God is good and we are not.

God could have sent everyone to hell and still be just and good, because we are the problem. We have sinned. But He did something else; something extraordinary. He sent His Son Jesus Christ to receive the punishment that we deserved because of our sins. Jesus came to earth and lived in this world without ever lying, without ever stealing, without being jealous or covetous, without sexual sin, and without doing any of the evil things we have done. At the age of thirty, He was baptized and when He came out of the water, the Spirit of God descended upon Him in the form of a dove and then the audible voice of God declared that Jesus was the Son of God. From then on, He healed the sick, delivered people from demons, and preached repentance, telling people to give up their sinful way of life and turn to God. Then He, who was without sin, was hung on a cross, was beaten, insulted, humiliated, and crucified, and He died.

If He had lied, stolen, hated anyone, or if He had sinned just once, He would have been guilty. But because Jesus was the only man who never sinned, three days later, He was resurrected. He conquered death so that we, through Him, could be forgiven for our sins and have a relationship with God. God is just and holy, so He could not let evil go unpunished. So, because He loved us, Jesus underwent the punishment in our place so that God's righteousness would be satisfied. He is alive today. He sits at the right hand of God and He sent His Holy Spirit down to earth.

Now what should we do? The Bible says that we must be born again: repent towards God, be baptized to Jesus Christ and receive the Holy Spirit. Repentance is when we recognize that we have sinned against a holy God, and that we are guilty before Him. It is when we turn away from sin, from our old way of life, and turn to God. Repentance is not just about confessing one's sins or feeling remorseful. Action always follows true repentance. A thief who repents stops stealing, a liar who repents stops lying. And we must put our faith in Jesus Christ, who paid the price for our sins on the cross. When we do this, something incredible happens. God takes away our heart of stone and gives us a new heart, a heart of flesh. It is like a new conscience. Over time, our heart has been stained by the evil things we have done, seen and heard. When we repent, God gives us a sharp and brand new conscience so that we can distinguish between good and evil. But this is not enough, we need to be baptized.

Baptism consists of two things: washing away our sins and burying our old life. Jesus said that he who sins is a slave to sin. You can compare it to the law of gravity. If I take something and drop it, it falls. And even if I believe that it won't fall, it will still fall because of the law of gravity. It is the same with sin: there is a spiritual law and when we begin to sin, we become slaves to it and we will always fall back into it. When we repent and get a new heart from God, we want to do what is right, but we can't because we are still bound to sin. That is why we need to be baptized. In water baptism, we die with Christ and we are set free from the power of sin. We bury our old life in the water and come out of the water as a new creation. We both die with Christ and are resurrected with Christ. Now washed clean from our sins, we are like Adam and Eve in the beginning before they sinned against God.

But this is still not enough. We need to be filled with the Holy Spirit. The Holy Spirit is the Spirit of God and He is the same Spirit that Jesus had when He was here on earth. He is the one who shows us our sin, who helps us to live a holy life, who leads us, teaches us, corrects us, comforts us, and supports us. It is this Spirit that Jesus promised to send down to earth so that we are not alone. When someone is filled with the Holy Spirit, they speak in a new language, which the Bible refers to as "speaking in tongues."

Before returning to God, Jesus, in Mark 16, said to his disciples:

Go into all the world and proclaim the gospel to the whole creation. Whoever believes and is baptized will be saved, but whoever does not believe will be condemned. And these signs will accompany those who believe: in my name they will cast out demons; they will speak in new tongues; they will pick up serpents with their hands; and if they drink any deadly poison, it will not hurt them; they will lay their hands on the sick, and they will recover." Now, as disciples of Christ, it is our responsibility to obey Jesus and do these things.

Jesus will come back soon and He will judge the world. Those who live in sin and have remained rebellious to God will be thrown into the lake of fire, where they will suffer for eternity. Those whose sins have been washed away and who belong to Him will live with Him and they will have access to the tree of life and live forever. Then, once again, everything will be good and perfect like it was in the very beginning.

God wants all of us to be saved and to have a relationship with Him. That is why He sent Jesus to die on the cross. But just like He gave Adam and Eve the freedom to choose between Him and sin, He gives us the same choice. He longs for a relationship with us, but He lets us choose if we want Him.

Now, back to our chess game. Remember: God created you. You have sinned. God sent Jesus Christ to die for your sin. So, what are you going to do?

www.phobiescolaire.fr